WHO TAKES
BRITAIN
TO WAR?

WHO TAKES BRITAIN TO WAR?

JAMES GRAY MP
AND MARK LOMAS QC

The
HISTORY
Press

First published 2014

The History Press
The Mill, Brimscombe Port
Stroud, Gloucestershire, GL5 2QG
www.thehistorypress.co.uk

British Library Cataloguing in Publication Data.
A catalogue record for this book is available from the British
Library.

ISBN 978 0 7509 6182 0

Typesetting and origination by The History Press
Printed in Great Britain

CONTENTS

ACKNOWLEDGEMENTS

This book was inspired by the work I did on a mid-term thesis as a student at the Royal College of Defence Studies in 2003. It was entitled 'Crown vs Parliament: Who decides to go to War?'[1] I am immodestly proud that it won a silver model of the RCDS 'beast' as a prize, and was published in the *Seaford House Papers*. It was written shortly after Tony Blair gave the House of Commons a vote on hostilities against Saddam Hussain.

Major General Keith Cima was my inspiration and mentor at RCDS, and General Sir Tim Granville-Chapman made many suggestions for improvements to that paper, and has also kindly contributed a foreword to this book.

I am indebted to the House of Commons Library, in particular to Claire Mills and Richard Kelly, whose detailed research papers, *Parliamentary Approval for Deploying the Armed Forces: An Introduction to the Issues*,[2] and an update to it in February 2013, I have quoted and used extensively. Richard Kelly also kindly read the final draft of the text, and corrected a number of details.

James de Waal's paper, 'Depending on the Right People, British Political-Military Relations, 2001–10',[3] which is a closely connected, but parallel, discussion to this one, made a particularly useful contribution to Chapter 8. The clerks and specialist advisers to the House of Commons Defence Committee, the Public Administration and Political and Constitutional Reform Select Committees and the House of

Lords Select Committee on the Constitution have had their work quarried extensively (as is largely acknowledged in the endnotes and bibliography).

My friend, Mark Lomas QC, contributed the fascinating historical insight in Part Three, as well as a host of corrections, suggestions and debates about the rest of it. Mark's robust conclusion to his historical section is a *cri de coeur* for constitutional stability. He is a true constitutional conservative and would much rather the system developed over centuries be retained. I, by contrast, regretfully acknowledge that there has been a fundamental change in the British Constitution, which has potentially devastating consequences for our ability to use military force in the future and that we must now do something about it if we are to maintain our role in world affairs.

I am grateful to Jacob Rees-Mogg MP, Madeleine Moon MP, Rt Hon. James Arbuthnot MP, Rosemary Fisher, Adam Fico, Anya Boulton and my wife, Philippa, for their detailed comments on the manuscript. Shaun Barrington and his colleagues at The History Press have been efficient, firm, unfailingly courteous and helpful. The errors and conclusions remain Mark Lomas' and my responsibility.

James Gray
House of Commons

FOREWORD

This is an important book. The events in August 2013, when Parliament was invited to vote on the appropriate action over the Syrian crisis, marked a turning point in our constitutional history, displacing the long-standing position that decisions over going to war are a matter for exercise of the Royal Prerogative, manifest these days in the Prime Minister and his cabinet. It is possible that few people in this country realised that so significant a change had happened. In an engaging way, James Gray explains what occurred and why and what it means. On the other hand, most people would recognise that conflict increasingly bears on this country's way of life in a global world, often feel threatened by the uncertainty it provokes, and that they are sometimes affected by the harm it brings. At the same time the emphasis on accountability for major decisions continues to grow, with the feeling that Parliament is often the means of achieving that goal. What is probably less understood is the extent to which decision-making that can lead to the lowest common denominator of agreement often serves the nation ill when its security is at stake. Many of those who threaten us, notably in the terrorist domain, are quick to exploit such weakness. So this book about strategic decision-making is timely. The early twenty-first-century solution to the dilemma we face between democratic accountability and the need to protect the nation will not be quick in coming, but this book sets the stage well for debate. It is to be hoped that responsible debate will follow – and soon. If it does not there is a real danger that we shall sleepwalk into a position where our influence in world affairs markedly declines, with far-reaching consequences for the well-being of the next generation.

General Sir Timothy Granville-Chapman
GBE, KCB, ADC Gen.

General Sir Timothy Granville-Chapman is a former Vice-Chief of the Defence Staff of the British Armed Forces. He presently holds the ceremonial position of Master Gunner, St James's Park.

INTRODUCTION

Who decides on Britain's wars? Who declares war, orders troops into action, commands them in action and decides how it's all going to end?

Originally it was the King; then the King in concert with the feudal barons. That slowly evolved into the King in Council; then, as Parliament increased its power, it evolved again into the King acting through his prime minister. After that, war-making powers devolved wholly to the Prime Minister and Cabinet. But the power they were exercising was always the same: the ancient 'Royal Prerogative' of the monarch to take his country to war.

Those powers had evolved in the British Constitution over many hundreds of years. Their use waxed and waned. Yet, as we hope to demonstrate in this book, the reliance on the Royal Prerogative in war-making survived pretty well unscathed into the twenty-first century.

Leaving aside for a moment the 2003 Iraq War, which was something of an anomaly, there was not much of an assault on its constitutional impregnability until 29 August 2013. That was the day on which Prime Minister David Cameron gave the House of Commons the final say over whether or not to launch an air strike against Syria. Leave aside, for the moment, the pretty universal view that any such strike would have been the wrong thing to do. The right outcome does not necessarily justify the wrong process leading to it. For, by allowing the House of Commons to have the final say in the matter, Mr Cameron ended the centuries-long convention that it should be the Prime Minster in Cabinet

IT IS ABSOLUTELY FORBIDDEN
TO CROSS THIS BORDER
INTO AFGHAN TERRITORY

'So ended the great war of 1878-80 ... We had 70,000 men in Afghanistan, and even then we really only held the territory within the range of our guns.' General Sir John Miller Adye.

who decides on war, albeit always ultimately answerable to Parliament for his decisions.

Now, it is perfectly true that the convention of the Royal Prerogative had been questioned by many parliamentarians and constitutional theorists for some time. It had become an increasingly common belief in recent years that taking the country to war was a matter that must be decided not by the monarch and his privy council, nor by the Prime Minister and his cabinet acting in the monarch's name, but more properly by the elected representatives of the people – Members of Parliament, sitting in the House of Commons.

Democrats and parliamentarians may well argue that a full and substantive debate on military intervention, such as that on 29 August 2013, has great advantages. Surely it is only right that MPs – the tribunes of the people – should have the final say over that most devastating of all decisions – to go to war? It is too grave and weighty a decision, they would argue, to leave to any one person. It must have collective approval or we should not do it; and Parliament is the ultimate distillation of the collective views of the nation. Surely it should therefore be Parliament who decides? What's more, this strengthens Parliament vis-à-vis the Executive, and as such can only be a good thing.

There is, of course, great strength in most of those arguments. Yet is it not at least possible that this apparent 'democratisation' of war may have long-term and extensive consequences for our ability as a nation to do what is right and necessary in military terms around the world? If, in future, it is backbench MPs who determine our military deployments overseas, will we ever make any? Will they be the right ones, and carried out with the speed and secrecy necessary to make them successful? All of these questions are critical to Britain's future role on the world stage.

So, David Cameron's apparently terminal abandonment of the use of the Royal Prerogative in war-making over Syria may well have wide-ranging constitutional, military and diplomatic consequences for Britain. This book

Gurkhas of 1RGR prepare for what became known as the 'Lam Death March', Operation Southern Scorpion, February 2008. In all, 400 troops would thrust into 3,000 square kilometres of Taliban territory north of Kandahar province. (Image courtesy of Nick Allen, from *Embed: To the End with the World's Armies in Afghanistan*)

will examine the development of war-making, from all-powerful medieval monarchs through unquestioned use of the Royal Prerogative by prime ministers, to this current fashion for democracy. It will consider how it happened, and the long-term consequences. It outlines some of the many possible downsides to excessive democracy in war-making; and it discusses the dilemma which these two competing pressures – democracy and military effectiveness – produce.

Finally, the outline of a solution is suggested, which would satisfy calls for democracy in war-making while still preserving the ability of the government to do what is right in the world.

PART ONE: WHO TAKES BRITAIN TO WAR NOW?

BY JAMES GRAY MP

1

X FACTOR WAR

Order, Order. The Ayes to the right were 272 and the Noes to the left were 285. So the Noes have it, the Noes have it.[1]

So it was that the Right Honourable John Bercow MP, Speaker of the House of Commons, announced on 29 August 2013 that rockets would *not* rain down on Syria the following weekend as the Prime Minister had apparently intended. Perhaps unknowingly, he was making constitutional history as he said it.

History has been 'made' in the chamber of the House of Commons on thousands of occasions over the centuries. Most of the great events in British history have been marked by important parliamentary debates and votes – wars; strikes; abdications; the creation of the National Health Service; budgets; Queen's Speech debates and the making or breaking of governments. Usually, these great and historic occasions are well noticed and marked by press and public alike. But just occasionally, parliamentary history is 'made' more or less unnoticed by parliamentarians or the wider world.

So it was on that Thursday, at 10.31 p.m. The House had been recalled for the specific purpose of agreeing to a limited American-led military strike against President Assad's regime in Syria. President Barack Obama had concluded that Assad had crossed a 'red line' by using chemical weapons against his own people. He planned to take military action against Syria as a result, and sought support from his oldest allies – Britain and France – in doing so. Their governments had apparently agreed in principle. But the UK Prime Minister, David Cameron, was mindful of promises he had made some years previously (in Opposition) that he would never take the country to war without the explicit approval of the House of Commons. In a speech as Leader of the Opposition in 2006, for example, Mr Cameron had said:

> I believe the time has come to take a look at those powers exercised by Ministers under the Royal Prerogative. Giving Parliament a greater role in the exercise of these powers would be an important and tangible way of making government more accountable. Just last week we first heard about the government's decision to send 4,000 troops to Afghanistan in the pages of the *Sun* newspaper … [2]

He was referring to the deployment into the Sangin area of Afghanistan's Helmand Province which, unannounced to Parliament, had occurred the previous week.

The Democracy Task Force he had established to look into the matter reported on 6 June the following year:

> We believe that it is no longer acceptable for decisions of war and peace to be a matter solely for the Royal Prerogative. The Democracy Task Force therefore recommends that a Parliamentary Convention should be established that Parliamentary assent – for example, the laying of a resolution of the House of Commons – should be required in timely fashion before the commitment of any troops … [3]

During the very recent parliamentary debate on the deployment of forces in Libya on 21 March 2011, the Foreign Secretary, William Hague, had gone one step further:

We will also enshrine in law for the future the necessity of consulting Parliament on military action.[4]

So by August 2013, and despite his (presumably con-ditional) promise to Barack Obama that the UK would assist with the deployment of military force in Syria, David Cameron really had no choice but to consult Parliament on the matter. In doing so, he was breaching many hundreds of years of practice; he was establishing what could be a dangerous precedent for the future; and he was taking a substantial political gamble – and one which he in fact lost. For, until that evening, surprising as it may seem, going to war had never before been subject to formal parliamentary approval (with the possible exception of the debates just prior to the start of the Iraq War in 2003).

Yet on this occasion, Mr Cameron insisted that, irre-spective of the merits and demerits of a strike against Syria, it could only be sanctioned by a substantive vote in the House. He recalled parliamentarians a few days early from their summer recess, in the hope of securing the authority he needed to support our oldest ally in their plan. Yet in doing so, he cannot have taken proper account of public opinion, nor of how that would be reflected in the views of the MPs of his own party. The tide of British public opinion, still scarred by Iraq and Afghanistan, was running strongly against military intervention anywhere else in the world, and the returning backbenchers, on Wednesday 28 August, were well aware of it. Even the most hawkish of Tory MPs, and even those in the safest of safe Conservative seats, would have been keenly aware of local opinion; of the threat from UKIP; and of the risk of non-reselection by their own Conservative Associations if they did not do the right thing. We can only imagine that David Cameron personally supported air strikes against Assad, and that he blithely thought that his backbench-ers would be of like mind. He could not have been more wrong in that judgement.

It is widely assumed – although not proven in documents – that the Prime Minister was planning to table a parliamentary motion approving such air strikes or other military action against Assad. Military assets of various kinds had been deployed to Cyprus and elsewhere already, and there was a widespread presumption in military circles that action was imminent – in the air if not (yet) on the ground. The use of chemical weapons was widely decried, and Labour's Ed Miliband had indicated in television interviews that Labour would support such government action. Had that been the case, the recall of Parliament would have been largely symbolic, parliamentarians no doubt simply using the occasion to publicly reiterate their abhorrence of the use of these vile weapons, and the Prime Minister duly being given authority to act alongside the US in punishing Assad for his use of them. Given Labour's presumed support for the motion, it must have seemed a relatively straightforward piece of parliamentary and political manoeuvring, and American and British rockets could have started to land on specified targets within Syria by the following weekend.

It was not to be. Smelling the political coffee, Mr Miliband conducted a last minute U-turn and announced that the Labour Party would not be supporting the government nor any kind of military action against Syria. Without Labour, and with Mr Cameron's Lib. Dem. coalition partners split and vacillating on the matter, only a handful of Tory dissidents would mean that the Prime Minister would lose the vote on any such motion.

No public records exist of the meetings which must have occurred that day between the Prime Minister and the Conservative Chief Whip, Sir George Young, but there can be little doubt that the 'Chief' would have been frank about the scant likelihood of securing a Commons majority for military action in Syria, since Labour were now lining up with Tory rebels to oppose it.

'Prime Minister, you are risking a humiliating defeat over this,' Sir George would have said. 'There is no precedent for a Prime Minister losing a parliamentary vote called to approve his decision to go to war. We have recalled Parliament, and so to face such a humiliation is a very high-risk strategy.'

Perhaps as a result of such advice as that, and as a result of the very many meetings which he himself had with unhappy backbenchers on the subject, the Prime Minister was forced to water down the motion he laid before Parliament that Thursday. It would now merely decry Assad's use of chemical weapons; it would call for the UN Inspectors to be allowed to visit the sites in question; it would demand talks in Geneva; and crucially it would promise a further House of Commons vote prior to any possible British military involvement.

The formal motion read:

That this House:
Deplores the use of chemical weapons in Syria on 21 August 2013 by the Assad regime, which caused hundreds of deaths and thousands of injuries of Syrian civilians;

Recalls the importance of upholding the worldwide prohibition on the use of chemical weapons under international law;

Agrees that a strong humanitarian response is required from the international community and that this may, if necessary, require military action that is legal, proportionate and focused on saving lives by preventing and deterring further use of Syria's chemical weapons;

Believes, in spite of the difficulties in the United Nations [whose Security Council had failed to reach unanimous resolution to take action, thanks to vetoes from Russia and China], that a United Nations process must be followed as far as possible to ensure the maximum legitimacy for any such action;

Believes that the United Nations Security Council must have the opportunity to [consider the briefing from their investigating team on the ground in Syria] and that every effort must be taken to secure a Security Council

Resolution backing military action before any such action is taken;

Notes that before any direct British involvement in such action a further vote in the House of Commons will take place;

And notes that this Resolution relates solely to efforts to alleviate humanitarian suffering by deterring use of chemical weapons and does not sanction any action in Syria with wider objectives.[5]

It is hard to know how any Parliamentarian could have objected to such a watered-down motion, yet Labour felt the necessity to table its own counter-motion. It read:

This House:
Expresses its revulsion at the killing of hundreds of civilians in Ghutah, Syria on 21 August 2013;

Believes that this was a moral outrage;

Recalls the importance of upholding the worldwide prohibition on the use of chemical weapons;

Makes clear that the use of chemical weapons is a grave breach of international law;

Agrees with the UN Secretary General that UN weapons inspectors must be able to report …

Supports steps to provide humanitarian protection to the people of Syria but will only support military action involving UK forces if and when the following conditions have been met:

That the weapons inspectors must have concluded their work and reported to the Security Council; there must be compelling evidence … The UN Security Council must have voted on it; that there is a clear legal basis for taking collective military action …; that such action must be legal, proportionate and time-limited;

and that the PM must report back to the House on the achievement of these conditions so that the House can vote on UK participation in such action … [6]

This counter-motion is, of course, astonishingly similar to the government motion. It is pretty anodyne, and crucially also calls for a second House of Commons vote before any action. It can only have been tabled for straightforward party political reasons – so that Labour could try to position itself as the anti-war party, presumably in the hope that commentators would not actually bother to read the precise terms of either their or the government's motions.

It is hard to understand why any parliamentarian, no matter how 'dovelike' and anti-war they may have felt, could possibly have objected to either motion. It is even harder to know why the Conservatives voted against the Labour motion, which was as easy on the eye as their own. Nonetheless, for reasons best known to their whips, the Coalition voted down the Labour motion; and then Labour and the Tory rebels voted down the government motion. So, quite contrary to urban memory of the occasion, the House of Commons ended up accepting no motion at all on Syria, despite the fact that both would have been so very easy to accept by any sensible person.

The following historic – if largely ignored – exchange then occurred at 10.31 p.m., just after Mr Speaker had announced the result of the vote:

> Edward Miliband: 'On a point of order, Mr Speaker. There having been no motion passed by this House tonight, will the Prime Minister confirm to the House that, given the will of the House that has been expressed tonight, he will not use the Royal Prerogative to order the UK to be part of military action before there has been another vote in the House of Commons?'

> The Prime Minister: 'Mr Speaker, I can give that assurance. Let me say that the House has not voted for either motion tonight. I strongly believe in the need for a tough response to the use of chemical weapons, but I also believe

in respecting the will of this House of Commons. It is very clear tonight that, while the House has not passed a motion, the British Parliament, reflecting the views of the British people, does not want to see British military action. I get that, and the Government will act accordingly.'[7]

This brief exchange, late one Thursday evening, is of huge importance in so many different ways. The least important but most intriguing element is the baffling illogicality of both men's argument that, despite the House of Commons having come to no formal resolution, it was somehow nonetheless clear that the House was opposed to war. After all, for all we know, some members may have been opposed to the UK being involved on any basis; some may have been in favour of immediate air-strikes but opposed to UN involvement; some may even have been opposed to the principle of putting the matter to a motion. We will never know. How either party leader was able to divine the 'will of the House' from the rejection of both motions remains a mystery. Yet, however they came to be uttered, the consequences for the history of the Middle East as a whole, and for Syria in particular, of these unscripted remarks late at night after such an astonishing parliamentary shambles, are yet to be calculated.

For there then followed a series of more or less haphazard events in London and Washington. Prompted by the Commons vote on that historic evening – or perhaps seizing on it as a way of escaping from a possibly rash threat against Assad (what one official later described as his 'get out of jail free card') – President Obama confirmed that he too would seek the support of Congress for military action. While waiting for Congress to be in session, Secretary of State Kerry made an apparently off-the-cuff remark to the effect that he would accept Syrian chemical disarmament if it was supervised by Russia. Russia and Syria indicated that they would be content with that, which allowed President Obama to avoid any vote in Congress; and indeed to avoid war. Diplomatic negotiations amongst the various parties ensued in Geneva;

Syria allowed access to most of their chemical weapons sites by inspectors; the chemical weapons were (we hope) largely destroyed; and a military strike with potentially global consequences was avoided – at least for now.

It appeared that the pacifist will of the people of the UK, expressed by their MPs in two negative votes – and the failure of the House to come to any very clear conclusion – had led to a respite for Syria from Allied retribution. (A subsequent reopening of negotiations with Iran over their nuclear ambitions may also be indirectly linked.)

Leaving aside the immediate diplomatic and military consequences of these events, 29 August 2013 also had significant and historic consequences for the British Constitution, for our standing in the world, and for our future ability to take any kind of military action. Mr Cameron's conceding a substantive parliamentary vote on whether or not to embark on military action before it took place may well have profound consequences for Britain's foreign policy and global positioning and ability to act for the good in the future.

Alistair Burt, the then Foreign Office Minister with responsibility for the Middle East, was interviewed by the *Guardian* on Monday 30 December, and described the consequences of the events of 29 August as:

> A constitutional mess in which the Commons can be guaranteed to back intervention only to defend the Falkland Islands and Gibraltar … I think we can assume those. I am not sure that we can assume anything else. Where does that leave us and our partnerships around the world?[8]

> We have put ourselves in a Constitutional mess this way. I think Government needs to take executive action in foreign affairs. It informs Parliament. If Parliament does not ultimately go for it, then the issue becomes a vote of confidence issue. I don't think you can handle foreign affairs by having to try to convince 326 people [a majority of MPs] each time you need to take a difficult decision.

You do it and if they don't like it they can vote you out and they can have a general election.

As we will describe in later chapters, this is a brief but accurate summary of the nature and extent of parliamentary control over a war-making process that had held good from at least March 1782 until August 2013.

Alistair Burt's comments run directly counter to the earlier view expressed by his close ally, William Hague, who had promised legislation to enshrine the right of Parliament to decide. One wonders if Mr Burt's conversion, despite the clear view of his erstwhile boss, may be a post-Syria 'straw in the wind'. It may yet be that Mr Cameron and Mr Hague will come to regret their pre-election promise to consult the House of Commons on going to war. We shall see.

It was certainly interesting to see an unnamed 'senior Foreign Office source' quoted in the same *Guardian* article:

> ... Voicing the hope that Britain would not lose its ability to act militarily and diplomatically ... Two key reasons for our diplomatic strength are our status as one of the five permanent members of the UN Security Council ... and our ability to be more flexible, adaptable and nimble than others – both diplomatically and militarily. I really hope that the lesson from August's parliamentary vote is that however we take decisions about military action in the future, we do so in a way that preserves rather than constrains our comparative advantage (or our ability to be nimble).

This was another brief, accurate and deadly summary of the potential effect of the ill-considered and mismanaged proceedings on the floor of the House of Commons on that shambolic August evening.

Since 1782, when Prime Minister Lord North had resigned after a complex series of negotiations over reinforcing our troops in the American War of Independence[9], prime ministers of all shades engaged in a variety of military activities without formally consulting Parliament. As an illustration, it may surprise you to learn that 1968 is the only year since 1945 in which no British service person has been killed on active service. Yet none of those wars were formally approved by a vote in Parliament before they had commenced. How can that have occurred? How can Prime Ministers over a period of at least 231 years – and monarchs for centuries before that – have engaged in such a wide variety of wars and military engagements without risking a Cameron-style parliamentary defeat over them? Is it that all of those wars and engagements were popular? Surely not. Perhaps previous Parliaments have been more subservient and respectful to the Prime Minister? But that 231 years spans the high tide of parliamentary scrutiny and control of the Executive. Perhaps the cases for going to war were clearer and stronger than that advanced by Mr Cameron with regard to Syria? Hardly likely.

The reason is none of these. It is simply that for the last 231 years or so, Prime Ministers have taken the country to war more or less unilaterally, and certainly without seeking a substantive Commons vote on the matter, using the Royal Prerogative – the very power that monarchs used for centuries before that. The Boer War, the First and Second World Wars, Korea, Suez, the Falklands, the Balkans, the Gulf War and even Afghanistan, all took place without any formal approval by Parliament. It was not until Iraq in 2003 that ministers first allowed a substantive vote on going to war, and even then it was a vote whose outcome was pretty predictable, at least partly because it was allowed only a couple of days before the actual outbreak of hostilities. Few observers would conclude from the precedent of Iraq that a parliamentary vote approving a war necessarily makes that a good war to have waged!

There were no further parliamentary votes on warfare after Iraq in 2003. There was no vote on the Helmand deployment in Afghanistan; and the parliamentary vote on the campaign in Libya in 2011 was on the Monday, the campaign having started on the previous Saturday.

Perhaps even more surprisingly, there was no vote on the huge new operation in 2006 which took our troops from the relatively safe area around Camp Bastion and Lashkar Gah in the south of Helmand Province into the much more dangerous area around Sangin, which also involved a significant increase in numbers of troops deployed. That deployment northwards was the subject of the report in the *Sun* newspaper to which David Cameron had referred in calling for greater parliamentary scrutiny.

In a recent study, the commentator James de Waal claims that ministers were not even informed, far less consulted, on the Sangin deployment. In his evidence to the House of Commons Defence Committee's enquiry into Afghanistan, the then Secretary of State for Defence, Des Browne, said that this decision 'was all briefed to me retrospectively and it has subsequently been described by those who were in command in military terms as an operational decision and that is how I perceived it'. He went on to say that he took responsibility for the decision as Secretary of State, but he did not know how the decision was taken nor on what precise grounds. By any standards that must be an astonishing admission for a Defence Secretary, with regard to one of the biggest decisions taken in either Iraq or Afghanistan, and it could not be further away from David Cameron's decision to take the potential Syrian action to a vote of the House.

In short, it was a long-established and crucially important constitutional principle that the Prime Minister could take the nation to war without any formal approval by Parliament, and the Syria vote on 29 August 2013 was the first occasion on which that principle had been truly breached. It was the first time in recent history that a parliamentary vote on war really mattered, and would genuinely affect the outcome.

Now one could argue that this was real evidence of the legislature clawing back some of its powers from the Executive;

and that of all matters, the act of going to war should be a matter for MPs and the people they represent. Yet the bigger question must be whether or not a parliamentary veto of this kind is necessarily the best thing for the peace of the world? The decision taken on 29 August 2013 with regard to Syria probably was the right one. Yet would that always be the case? Might the precedent it established not have dangerous consequences for Britain's place in the world?

On both sides of the Atlantic, the TV programme *X Factor* is currently commanding record audiences. A series of performers – ranging from the wholly untalented through to the competent yet undiscovered – perform in a gruelling series of tests in front of a panel of self-appointed 'celebrities' led by Simon Cowell. *Strictly Come Dancing* has similarly emerged from its Blackpool Winter Gardens ballroom dancing obscurity as a clash of celebrity titans performing a series of ever more acrobatic routines in the good name of 'dancing'. Both programmes, and many like them, offer the final say to the people. The masses use the phone-in to 'vote' for their favourites. The most popular (irrespective of any possible artistic merit) wins, with the most profound consequences and untold wealth for the winner. It's not a talent show. It's the modern equivalent of the Roman amphitheatre and, like it, beloved by the populace. The people scream their approval or otherwise and the Emperor (the presenter) signifies that the performers will live or die by a 'thumbs up' or 'thumbs down' signal.

The populist – if no doubt perfectly correct – decision of the House of Commons not to launch strikes against Syria on 29 August 2013 bears real similarities to *X Factor* and *Strictly*. The decision was not based on the best available intelligence; it was not the result of careful diplomatic thought and negotiation; it was not the result of brilliant academic analysis. The decision not to launch a strike against Assad was taken for none of those reasons. It was taken simply because any such strike would have been unpopular with the people.

Is this really the best way for Britain to decide whether or not to go to war? We appear to be at risk of entering an era of 'X Factor Warfare'.

Backbench MPs in the House of Commons will rarely, if ever, vote for any kind of military action, no matter how justifiable it may be, unless they can be certain that it will be popular with their electorate. They are seeking re-election, quite possibly within a short time of the proposed military action. Their majority may well be tiny by comparison with the representations they have received on the matter. If you have a majority of 100 votes, 1,000 letters opposing something fairly concentrates the mind!

So, if our representatives are to be asked to vote for (or against) warfare, there must be at least a good possibility that the test for going to war will become, not necessity, but popularity. Only those wars (if there are such things) which are 'popular' will be waged. Those which may be perfectly justifiable and vitally necessary for the interests of the country, but are unpopular, will not. This would be a form of 'X Factor Warfare'. Parliament are the celebrity judges. The people – by their vote – will decide whether or not to go to war – 'Dial 1 for war and destruction; Dial 2 for world peace; Press # to register your vote.'

So how have we got here, and what, at least in the UK, are the consequences for the future?

This book will examine the use of war-making powers under the Royal Prerogative. It will trace the historic development of them; it will consider what the consequences for world history have been as a result of their use; it will ask what would be the consequences for Britain's place in the world of their abandonment; it will consider what rebalancing of the executive/parliamentary see-saw would result from it; and it will seek to provide a solution which strengthens Parliament, while at the same time giving the Prime Minister and his Cabinet the powers which they need to ensure the defence of the realm, and the promotion of good in the wider world.

2

CAN WAR BE DEMOCRATIC?

Despite their Royal Prerogative powers, prime ministers have always, of course, been politically answerable to Parliament. If they were to have engaged in wrong, unjustified, or even unsuccessful military adventures overseas, their support in the House of Commons would evaporate; they would doubtless lose any subsequent Vote of No Confidence, and their prime ministerial careers would be at an end.[1]

So, quite leaving aside the technicalities about what they may or may not be allowed to do under the (unwritten) constitution, the Executive have always been subject to political pressures and risks. That, of course, remains the case even post-Syria. David Cameron's standing was without doubt damaged by his apparent, if unsuccessful, attempt to engage in military action against Assad. It was poor political judgement.

But for the moment, let us leave those political realities to one side and drill down into the constitutional legalities and technicalities of going to war. The litmus test of who it is who historically has 'taken Britain to war' must be whether the Prime Minister 'informs' Parliament of his war-making decision (often after the start of the action), or whether he 'consults' Parliament about it. The latter, of course, would imply that his military intentions could be thwarted by the will of the House, as they were over Syria.

Prime ministerial 'announcements' (Second World War) or 'statements' (Falklands, Afghanistan) are plainly informative. So-called Private Notice Questions (Korea, Afghanistan), and adjournment debates (*passim*) merely give parliamentarians the opportunity to express their views on the matter. No vote is possible on them, and while they may give the PM a flavour of opinion in the House and the country, they are incapable of thwarting his will. They are mechanisms by which he 'informs' the House of his military intentions.

By contrast, full-scale substantive debates culminating in a vote (Iraq, 2003 and Syria, 2013) are without doubt 'consultative' in a very real way. If such a vote is lost, the Prime Minister cannot realistically commit troops, no matter how overwhelming the national interest may be. That is why, until the Iraq 2003 experience, there were no such substantive debates culminating in a vote prior to committing troops to war, and nor does there seem to have been much complaint about the matter.

At the turn of the twenty-first century, things were about to change. As the 2003 Iraq War approached, the principle behind the Royal Prerogative began to face some pretty fundamental questioning by such constitutional thinkers as William Hague, the rebel Labour backbencher Graham Allen, and the late Tony Benn. In 1999, for instance, Tony Benn had said:

> Every Prime Minister needs the Monarchy to give him or her the executive power to do all things that Prime Ministers can do. It is interesting that Prime Ministers get their Legislative majority from the electors and their executive powers from the Crown.
>
> The Prime Minister has assumed the power of a president, using the Royal Prerogatives that have survived since the middle ages, his huge parliamentary majority and his tight control of the Labour Party machine to be sure he always gets his way ... The divine right to rule has merely been transferred from Buckingham Palace to Number 10 Downing Street.[2]

The Public Administration Select Committee launched an enquiry into 'Ministerial Powers and Prerogative' in April 2003 to examine the 'gaps that existed in ministerial accountability for prerogative powers'.[3] Their terms of reference were instructive:

> [Some people say] the Prerogative gave Ministers too free a hand. The current [Labour] Government had, when in Opposition, made clear that it felt that the prerogative needed at the very least radical change – or abolition. It was seen as very doubtful whether the prerogative was compatible with democracy. Against this view, it could be argued that the prerogative provided the flexibility and capacity for action required by governments faced with a complex and dangerous modern world.

Its chairman, Dr Tony Wright, was quoted as saying:

> It is time to re-examine this strange state of affairs, which means that vital functions of our government, from the power to run the civil service to the power to deploy troops at home and abroad, rest on uncertain and antique foundations. Few other countries have such opaque constitutional arrangements. No one doubts that ministers need to have effective executive powers, but it is vital that Parliament has a chance to scrutinise them properly before they are exercised.

Further evidence of the way history was moving comes from a transcript of William Hague and Tony Benn in conversation on the radio. Hague said:

> You know people would get very cross in Parliament if war was started without a vote or any debate. Although governments can still in theory go to war with the royal prerogative, in practice I don't think they can. In the Gulf War, in Kosovo, and now over the Iraqi situation,

Parliament has always had a debate, or a series of debates, and we've been able to say what we think, so I don't think it's a big problem in practice. [He was actually incorrect about the Gulf War and Kosovo.][4]

Tony Benn replied:

Why doesn't the House of Commons assert itself? ... Bush, under the US Constitution, has to go to the House of Representatives and the Senate to give him authority to go to war ... There is nothing like the importance of sending British servicemen into war, who might be killed, with their MP, who they are free to elect, having no say whatsoever on whether they should go to war. [Tony Benn was equally inaccurate in his understanding of the US War Powers Act, which simply demands subsequent approval of military action within three months of deployment.]

Soon afterwards, the *House Magazine* was reporting Tony Benn as saying:

The Executive have given the House a vote on a substantive motion on Iraq almost as an act of generosity. But such votes need codifying so that parliamentary approval is required for war, for the ratification of treaties.[5]

The mood of the moment was also reflected in the speeches and writing of sacked Labour whip, Graham Allen. He had previously issued a controversial and rebellious – but perfectly accurate – book about the increasingly presidential nature of Mr Blair's premiership, and about the consequent decline in Parliament's primacy. He argued – quite convincingly – that the over-mighty Charles I had had his powers transferred more or less directly to an over-mighty Tony Blair. Graham Allen now became a focus for those demanding that Parliament should have the right to approve action against Iraq. His War Making Powers (Parliamentary Approval of the Commitment of UK Armed Forces to Hostilities Abroad) Motion (Early Day Motion 733) – which could not become law but which may be a useful litmus test of parliamentary opinion, being signed by some 148 MPs – read, inter alia:

> Parliament shall ... approve the ... commitment of armed forces to hostilities abroad ... before such a commitment is made ... or at least within 20 days of a deployment; the Prime Minister will present a report to Parliament ... setting out the circumstances necessitating the commitment, ... its extent, chain of command, and anticipated scope and duration ...[6]

Graham Allen subsequently made public the text of his letter to the Government Chief Whip, to explain his rebellion over the Iraq War:

> Dear Chief Whip, ... I have received a PLP [Parliamentary Labour Party] pager message from you telling me that 'there is a 3-line whip on Labour MPs to vote for a motion on Iraq', although I have not been given the courtesy of being told what that motion is. If it is to commit British troops to war against Iraq, I will not support it ... Those who advise the Prime Minister on Parliamentary tactics [i.e. the Chief Whip!] have not served him well ... by refusing to give Parliament the democratic right (rather than by grace and favour) to debate the issue. Parliament has been treated with contempt – another crowd control exercise rather than as a body which has at least as much legitimacy to speak for the people of our country as the Prime Minister has to govern it ... This will bring Government and Parliament further into disrepute.[7]

In January 2003, Prime Minister Blair had told the Liaison Committee:

I cannot think of a set of circumstances in which a
Government can go to war without the support of
Parliament ... The reality is that in the end Governments
are accountable to Parliament ... and they are accountable
for any war they engage in, as they are for anything else.[8]

He went on to appear to accept that it would be right for
Parliament to vote:

There is a right to vote. The question is, do you take
one step further and get rid of the Royal Prerogative?
I do not see any reason to change it, but I do really
think that in the end it is more theoretical than real,
this issue, because the truth is that ... if in relation to
any conflict ... Parliament voted down the Government
... it is just not thinkable that the Government would
then continue the conflict. That has been the case all
the way through. So I think that even though it may
be strictly true to say that the Royal Prerogative means
you do it and in strict theory, Parliament is not the
authority, in the end Parliament is the authority for any
government. ... I mean, can you honestly imagine a set
of circumstances in which the Government is defeated
by Parliament on a conflict and says 'Well, I'm just
ignoring that?'

So in a 'Blairite' and rather tortured sort of way, he seemed
to be acknowledging demands for greater democratic
involvement in war-making, while still seeking to make the
argument for the use of the Royal Prerogative.

The then Foreign Secretary, Jack Straw, had in November
2002 seen the need for a substantive debate if military action
were taken against Iraq. Interestingly, he had said as early as
1994, in a Labour Party policy document, that:

The Royal Prerogative has no place in modern western democracy ... [The Prerogative] has been used as a

smoke-screen by Ministers to obfuscate the use of power for which they are insufficiently accountable.[9]

That was in Opposition, and his tone had rather changed when he was in government. Now he stressed that:

> ... It might not be possible to have such a debate in advance of action, if the consequent loss of the element of surprise were to put service personnel in danger.[10]

In a contemporary note, the House of Commons Library questioned whether:

> Those who call for debates on substantive motions [could] contemplate the House being given an opportunity to express an opinion on the Government's policy or being given a constitutional role in approving the recourse to military action.. It seems unlikely that the Government would wish to concede the prerogative in this area ...
>
> ... Today it is common for members with dissenting views to press for a debate on a substantive motion in order to record their view in a vote, and to create the opportunity to move amendments.[11]

So the constitutional thinking was without doubt moving on. The House of Commons Library was perhaps being a little unkind in seeming to argue that calls for substantive debates were little other than political rhetoric. After all, 148 backbenchers, most of them Labour, had signed Graham Allen's motion; there was some serious constitutional discussion emerging on the issue; and both the Foreign Secretary and the PM (albeit under pressure) seemed to have acknowledged the need for a substantive debate before any commitment of troops to war.

In the twelve months or so prior to the Iraq conflict in 2003, the Prime Minister nonetheless sought to preserve the Royal Prerogative by 'informing' rather than 'consulting' Parliament – at first. There was a general debate on 'Defence in the World' in which Iraq was extensively debated; one adjournment debate; and eight ministerial and prime ministerial statements in the month before the war, but still a very real reluctance to allow a substantive vote on the matter. But then, on 25 November 2002, the government entered uncharted constitutional waters when they finally conceded the first of three full-scale parliamentary debates on the subject, resulting in substantive votes. And that – for the first time ever – before the start of operations.

The first vote was on 25 November 2002, when the motion was:

> That this House supports UNSCR 1441 agrees that the Government of Iraq must comply fully with all provisions of the resolution; and that, if it fails to do so, the Security Council should meet in order to consider the situation.[12]

Those opposed to war under any circumstances proposed an amendment which was voted down by 452 to 85, the Opposition voting with the Labour government.
On 26 February 2003, the motion was:

> That this House takes note of Command Paper Cm 5769 on Iraq; reaffirms its endorsement of United Nations Security Council Resolution 1441 ... supports the Government's continuing efforts in the United Nations to disarm Iraq of its weapons of mass destruction; and calls upon Iraq to recognise that this is its final opportunity to comply with its disarmament obligations.[13]

An amendment to 'leave out from "destruction" to the end and add "but finds the case for military action against Iraq as yet unproven"' was supported by 122 Labour rebels, fifty-eight Liberals and others, and thirteen Tories – a total of 199.

It was, nonetheless, defeated by a combined Labour and Tory majority of 184 and the substantive motion was similarly passed by a majority of 310.

The important point is that for the first time ever, a total of 199 MPs – roughly a third of the total, and including something close to half of all government backbenchers – had effectively voted against going to war – or so they thought. Eighty-eight rebels in November, had become 199 by February and it was to be 217 by 18 March. On that day, just a couple of days before the action actually started, the government allowed a full-scale substantive debate which – by anyone's standards – must be one of the most important parliamentary events in living memory, at least until 29 August 2013, and one with a particular constitutional significance.

The motion read, inter alia:

> That this House ... recognises that Iraq's weapons of mass destruction and long-range missiles, and its continuing non-compliance with UNSCRs, pose a threat to international peace and security ...; notes that ... Iraq has rejected the final opportunity to comply ...; notes the opinion of the Attorney General that ... the authority to use force under Resolution 678 has revived; ... supports the decision of Her Majesty's Government to use all means necessary to ensure the disarmament of Iraq's weapons of mass destruction; ... and offers wholehearted support to the men and women of Her Majesty's forces ...[14]

Tony Blair opened this most memorable debate by saying:

> At the outset, I say that it is right that the House debate this issue and pass judgement. That is the democracy that is our right, but that others struggle for in vain. Again I say that I do not disrespect the views in opposition to mine ... Here we are, the government with their most

serious test, their majority at risk, the first Cabinet resignation ... the main parties internally divided ... This is a
debate that, as time has gone on, has become less bitter,
but no less grave.[15]

Iain Duncan Smith said:

The House and the whole country rightly recognise that
we are soon likely to be at war ... The Opposition recognise the heavy responsibility that the Prime Minister and
the government have to bear ... I make it clear from the
outset that the Opposition will vote tonight in the same
lobby as the government ...

This time, 217 people – the largest rebellion in parliamentary history – voted for the amendment which would have
added a postscript to the main motion that '[This House]
believes that the case for war against Iraq has not yet
been established, especially given the absence of specific
UN authorisation ...' A further forty-seven abstained (the
author being one of them, being deeply opposed to war
with Iraq, but lacking the political courage to vote against
it – mea maxima culpa), 396 voted against the amendment,
and the unamended substantive motion was then won by
412 votes to 149.

So why did this fundamental change come about? Why
was it that Mr Blair conceded to backbench and Opposition
demands for a substantive debate? What was different
about the run-up to the Iraqi war compared to any other
conflict in living memory prior to that?

The difference was that there was no consensus about
the correctness, nor even the legal justification for such a
war. The Second World War, Korean War, Falklands War
and First Gulf War, as well as military action in such places
as Sierra Leone, Bosnia, Kosovo, and even to an extent
Northern Ireland, enjoyed a good degree of public and
parliamentary consensus about their necessity. In other

words, because on those occasions the nation had to a very large degree supported the Prime Minister's use of the Royal Prerogative, it was perfectly reasonable that he should make use of it. It really does not matter very much whether the government used prime ministerial statements, adjournment debates or even full parliamentary debates to allow discussion of it. The outcome of the discussion was easily predictable in advance.

But for the very first time, with the Iraq War (and the same would be found with regard to Syria more than ten years later) there was no such consensus. Indeed, there was a reasonable consensus against what the Prime Minister was seeking to do. A few days before the Iraq conflict, the polls suggested that 75 per cent of the people were opposed to it (compared to 70 per cent in favour of the Afghanistan operations). There were coordinated protests in many countries on 15 February 2003, with the estimates in London for the numbers taking part in a rally in Hyde Park varying between 750,000 and almost 2 million. It could even be argued that initial attempts to avoid consulting Parliament in a truly substantive way in itself contributed to undermining the public and Parliament's confidence in the correctness – or even the legality – of the war effort. If the need to go to war with Saddam was so obvious and overwhelming, why could not the government explain it properly to the people and to Parliament, including subjecting the decision to a vote? It was this question which was acknowledged by Tony Blair's rather belated decision to allow a full parliamentary debate.

So at a glance, the constitutional position is perfectly plain. Prior to committing troops, the Prime Minister had allowed Parliament to have a substantive vote on the matter for the first time ever – at least in a controversial war. Parliament voted 'yes' and we went to war. Had they voted 'no', the troops would have come home. There is no doubt, as the Prime Minister had previously acknowledged to Parliament, that this would have been the political reality.

The public unease about entry into the Iraq War was expressed in what was the biggest demonstration in British history on 15 February 2003 in Hyde Park. Something that tends to be forgotten in the UK is that the estimated 1 million protesters were part of a far bigger constituency that day – there were protests in more than 800 cities worldwide. The Chilcot Inquiry was announced on 15 June 2009.

But wearing the rose-tinted spectacles of the constitutional theorist, let us have a look again at the precise wording of the motion on which Parliament had voted. For the truth is that this motion does not – technically speaking – breach the Royal Prerogative.

The Foreign Office wordsmith who drafted it says that 'the authority to use force under Resolution 678 has revived', and so calls on the House to 'support the decision of HMG that the UK ...'[16] and goes on to offer wholehearted support to our troops in the traditional way. Those who voted against the motion (or in favour of the amendment) no doubt believed that they were voting against going to war. They certainly were in a political sense, but in a strict constitutional sense, even if the motion had fallen or the amendment had been passed the Prime Minister could still, strictly theoretically, have taken the country to war. So, from a constitutional purist's standpoint, it could be argued that this motion does not, in fact, damage the theory behind the Royal Prerogative at all. That apparently legalistic point may well prove an important defence were the Prime Minister's Royal Prerogative rights tested in a court of law in some future conflict.

But leaving aside that constitutional theorist's caveat for now, it is reasonable to conclude that there were three important and historic constitutional precedents set in the run-up to the Iraq War. First, unlike previous conflicts, it was a highly contentious war. Second, as a result of (or perhaps despite) its controversial nature, the government allowed three substantive debates and votes on the issue. Third, they all occurred before the outbreak of hostilities. So the reality is that the Prime Minister and Foreign Office fought a bit of rearguard action, but failed.

There can be no denying that the debates and the votes (particularly the vote on 18 March) were a substantial breach of the historic Royal Prerogative. The political – if not the strict constitutional theorist's – reality is that had the House voted against the motion, the Prime Minister would have had no option but to withhold our troops from action in Iraq. Neither the Parliamentary Labour Party, nor the Opposition, nor the country would have allowed the PM to 'go it alone'. After all, the PM would no longer have had the support of the House of Commons. A Motion of No Confidence would very likely have followed, and the Queen would doubtless have had to consider whether or not Mr Blair still had the constitutional right to exercise the

Royal Prerogative. The vote on 18 March 2003, without doubt, formed a substantial constitutional watershed.

One consequence of this constitutional precedent in 2003 has been the continued questioning of the use of the Royal Prerogative to go to war – at least partly as a result of the common perception that the Iraq War was unjustified, or even illegal. Several attempts were made to introduce a Private Member's Bill (a mechanism which virtually never succeeds) to the effect that a substantive parliamentary vote would be necessary before any possible deployment of troops. In 2007 the (Labour) government announced a package of constitutional reforms that would involve, amongst other things, limiting the use of the Royal Prerogative.

After a series of consultation papers, the government then brought forward its proposals in a White Paper in 2008. It stipulated that any request for deployment of troops should be by a Resolution of the House of Commons, preceded by a debate (with no vote) in the House of Lords; that the government should continue to be allowed to take action in an emergency to protect national security; that operations involving special forces should need no parliamentary authority; and that the Prime Minister should personally determine how much information should be laid before the House to seek approval for deployments.

Thinking within the Conservative Party was moving in a similar direction. David Cameron's Democracy Task Force published a paper in 2007 concluding, inter alia, that:

> We believe that it is no longer acceptable for decisions of war and peace to be a matter solely for the Royal Prerogative. We recommend that a Parliamentary Convention should be established that Parliamentary assent – for example the laying of a resolution in the House of Commons – should be required in timely fashion before any commitment of troops. Under conditions of dire emergency, this requirement could be waived with

the proviso that the Prime Minister must secure retro-spective Parliamentary approval.[17]

That would have the effect of bringing this country close to the position of the USA following their implementation of the War Powers Act 1973.

William Hague's evidence to the Public Administration Select Committee in 2003 went even further. He called for a statutory requirement for ministers to consult Parliament in cases of conflict, and sketched out the recent parliamentary history of British military interventions. He saw the Iraq 2003 vote as 'given to the House of Commons as a kind of act of generosity by the government for which we had to be grateful at the time'. Pointing out that there was no such substantive vote over the Kosovo crisis, he suggested that government goodwill was not enough:

> I think that it actually should be laid down in an Act of Parliament or in the Standing Orders of the House of Commons ... that the power to commit troops to action needs codifying, so that parliamentary approval is required before it takes place or as soon as possible thereafter ...[18]

Yet when the Conservative Party finally came to power (and in coalition with the Liberal Democrats, whose views on the Royal Prerogative were perhaps even more extreme and clear), they were faced with a number of military involve-ments and deployments for which they signally failed to change their reliance on the Royal Prerogative.

British participation in the Libya operation was announced on 18 March 2011, when Prime Minister Cameron simultaneously indicated that a Substantive Motion, seeking retrospective approval for the deploy-ment of forces, would be tabled on Monday 21 March. He said: 'I am sure that the House will accept that the situation requires us to move forward on the basis of the Security

Council Resolution immediately.'[19] The motion was indeed approved – by 557 votes to thirteen.

But was it really capable of having been defeated? Its defeat would have meant national humiliation with our troops having to withdraw; it would without a doubt have led to questions about the Prime Minister's decision, and very probably to some kind of a confidence motion against him. The political reality is that, just as in the debates immediately following the declarations of war in 1914 and 1939, there was no possibility of anything other than an overwhelming vote in support of the predetermined military action. So why is that any different, in reality, to the use of the Royal Prerogative at any time over the last 200 years and more, which was always dependant on tacit political support underlying the military action in question?

Next, on 14 January 2013, the government announced that military assets would be deployed to support the deployment of French military personnel and equipment to Mali. It was argued that this was an emergency response, and neither a substantive debate nor any vote was allowed. There was a degree of criticism of the lack of parliamentary approval, especially in view of the Conservative Party's oft-repeated view that there should be. Yet bizarrely enough, Andrew Lansley who, as Leader of the House, was forced to answer questions on the matter, would undertake only 'that the House be regularly and appropriately informed about our engagement in Mali and north-west Africa ...'[20]

He did go on to acknowledge the government's commitment 'that we will observe the existing convention that before UK troops are committed to conflict, the House of Commons should have an opportunity to debate and vote on the matter, except when there is an emergency ...' He went on:

One should also recognise that ... the role of British troops [in Mali] is clearly not a combat role and it is not our intention to deploy combat troops ... I would not carry the analogy to the point where the convention is engaged in the sense of a requirement for a debate and vote in this House.[21]

There was still no substantive vote allowed on our continuing involvement in Afghanistan – or indeed on our withdrawal, which David Cameron announced soon after coming to power in 2010, and which is almost as significant as our initial deployment. The only vote on Afghanistan throughout the ten or more years of our war there was on a motion before the so-called 'Backbench Business Committee'.

The coalition government had established this committee as a way of allowing substantive debates and votes on issues of key concern to backbench MPs. Within a few months of its establishment on 9 September 2010, the debate was on the motion 'That this House supports the continued deployment of UK Armed Forces in Afghanistan',[22] a motion which was passed by 310 votes to 14 – perhaps rather surprisingly given the mood in the country.

The legal, constitutional and political consequences of votes on Backbench Business Committee debates remain a matter of conjecture. For example on this occasion, had the House voted against the motion, what would have been the practical consequences of that action? No one really knows. There would plainly have been political pressure on the Prime Minister to take note of the will of the House, and his decisions about the way in which we end our involvement in Afghanistan may have been to a greater or lesser degree affected by it. Yet, what is absolutely certain is that he would not have felt any consequent necessity to withdraw our troops in anything like a short timeframe. The Backbench Business Committee simply does not have the authority to control the government in that way, so any such vote would have been indicative, at best.

In other words, the fact of the matter is that every single one of the military involvements of the last twenty years, up to and including Libya and Mali, have been undertaken by the Prime Minister and Cabinet under the Royal Prerogative. That realisation is in stark contrast with the continual statements from politicians of all kinds and all parties that they were determined to give Parliament the vote (e.g. William Hague: 'We will enshrine in law for the future the necessity of consulting Parliament on military action.').[23]

To be fair to the current coalition government, it is reported that they have a team of officials struggling to put some kind of 'War-Making Act' together. It is said that they are finding it very difficult to come up with any formulation of words which would allow the House of Commons a formal approval role, while at the same time providing the government with enough freedom to manoeuvre in an emergency. (Perhaps the outline of a solution proposed later in this book may help them!)

The reality they are facing is that the full and final abandonment of the Royal Prerogative in favour of parliamentary approval would mean that unless a proposed war passed a certain threshold of popularity – no matter how right it may be from a humanitarian or strategic standpoint – it won't happen. Wars would have to be popular to be waged. The worrying thing is that there may well be circumstances under which the least popular war may actually be the most necessary. There might even be occasions on which a popularly acclaimed war (if there is such a thing) was in fact the wrong thing to do.

That being the case, is there not at very least a strong and persuasive argument that the Prime Minister should still be empowered to take the country to war without the necessity of a popular vote in the House of Commons? Is it not right that he should continue to use the Royal Prerogative to go to war and to 'inform' rather than to 'consult' Parliament about it? After all, it is not true to argue that the Royal Prerogative gives the Prime Minister 'power without responsibility'. It actually gives him the power to act responsibly. Were a Prime Minister to seek to take the country to war without very extensive discussions and consultation with Parliament, or without MPs' tacit consent at least, his position would quickly become untenable. It is not 'Prime Ministerial Prerogative' which allows him to commit troops to war, it is 'Royal Prerogative' which he exercises simply because he commands a majority in the House of Commons. Prime ministerial use of the Royal Prerogative depends on trust – it depends on the people trusting him to use it properly and justly.

What we are talking about here is the difference between statesmanship and political expediency. The more Parliament is 'consulted' rather than 'informed' and the greater the need felt for some kind of parliamentary mandate for the Prime Minister's use of the Royal Prerogative, the less likely it is that the Prime Minister will necessarily be acting in the best interests of the nation as a whole and of international peace and security. You cannot mix statesmanship and political expediency – very often the two would be in direct conflict with one another.

Surely, the reality is that no matter how much they may protest to the contrary, ministers know perfectly well that warfare by the democratic will of the people, expressed through a formal vote in the House of Commons, is virtually impossible to achieve. Effective military action simply cannot be approved in advance by the House of Commons.

With all of that as background, we come to the extraordinary events surrounding the proposed military action against Syria in August 2013. David Cameron's recall of Parliament from its summer recess; the motion to strike against Syria; his watering down of that motion; his failure even then to achieve a majority; Labour's equal collapse; his illogical, if politically astute, announcement that war would not now proceed; and the subsequent national and international events, have all been previously described.

But the most astonishing outcome of it all is that this was the first time in recorded history that a Prime Minister had fully abandoned the Royal Prerogative; that he had asked for substantive support from the House of Commons before committing the country to military action; that he had then failed to achieve it; and that the action in consequence did not go ahead. This is an historic breach of the principles behind the Royal Prerogative of positively cosmic proportions and a constitutional innovation with potentially wide-ranging consequences for Britain's positioning on the world stage for generations to come.

PART TWO: WHO WILL TAKE BRITAIN TO WAR IN THE FUTURE?

BY JAMES GRAY MP

UN Security Council in session.

3

DEMOCRACY OR STRATEGY?

If, as we have described, military action were from now on to be a function of a democratically elected House of Commons, then what would be the strategic consequences of that constitutional change? What might be the geo-political, military and diplomatic consequences of this democratisation of warfare?

The first thing to be clear about is that unless we do something pretty radical about it, this constitutional precedent will be irreversible for any future Prime Minister. It is hard to imagine any act of war – including defending the realm against an aggressor – which would not have at least some degree of disagreement in the country and in Parliament. And it is hard to imagine, therefore, any Prime Minister being able to avoid offering a substantive vote; and that – crucially – in advance of any irreversible military commitment.

This may be a worthwhile blow for the supremacy of parliamentary democracy, but it may well have a number of most unwelcome consequences for the defence of the realm. There can be no doubt that it would delay decisions. Could the Prime Minister act without consulting Parliament to deal with an incoming intercontinental ballistic missile? Probably. But what if it were an overseas threat to our survival and prosperity, which swift and secret pre-emptive action might deter? For example, the deployment of Iranian vessels or weaponry aimed at closing the Straits of Hormuz might be avoided by a pre-emptive show of force. Would the PM really have time to discuss such a deployment in a substantive debate in the House of Commons, and how could he do so without giving away the necessary element of surprise?

The nature of decision-making within a reformed NATO may be affected by it. NATO Rapid Reaction Forces may require quicker political decision-making than previously, which the need for parliamentary support would scupper. What if a NATO or even EU Defence Force decision were to be subject to qualified majority voting, as some euro-enthusiasts are suggesting? Would a parliamentary veto be applicable – or a prime ministerial one? What would be the consequences if Parliament agreed to war, but the UN Security Council vetoed it, or vice versa? Would the UK ambassador to the UN take his orders from the Prime Minister or from Parliament?

To hamstring the government's freedom of action to this extent would inevitably have the effect of side-lining Britain on the world stage. In the post-cold war era, either you are with what Richard Perle describes as the 'posse' of the good guys headed by the white-hatted sheriff, the US, or you are left behind. Slavish concern over parliamentary views or majorities could make us miss the posse as it rides out.

It may affect our diplomatic stance on a number of issues. In the words of Frederick the Great, 'Diplomacy without arms is like music without instruments.' There might be small, localised wars – like Sierra Leone, for instance – which the House of Commons might unhelpfully delay or veto at the cost of innocent people's lives.

It might lead to the Prime Minister being more open with the intelligence available to him than he ought, in an effort to persuade the House, with obvious consequences both for the intelligence source and for the conduct of the action. Is it really right that backbenchers should have access to even the most secret of secret intelligence in order to judge whether or not military action is really necessary? They would also have to be given the full legal advice about the war; and they would have to develop the intellectual powers to make sense of it all. Or if the PM is not to be more open with the intelligence and legal advice available to him, might that not risk exacerbating the need to 'spin' the intelligence to persuade Parliament? Mr Blair's 'Dodgy Dossier' used to justify Iraq is a good example.

It would lead to an unwelcome politicisation of conflict. What would happen, for example, if the governing party were struggling to maintain a very slim parliamentary majority? Might not even the highest-minded Opposition be tempted to find party political advantage? If those who are to take the final decision about whether or not to go to war are backbenchers who are seeking re-election, quite possibly within a short space of time, then almost by definition, they will politicise what really ought to be an entirely non-political decision. MPs will only vote for those military engagements which are absolutely obvious, and more or less popular. Wars which – often for very good, if secret, reasons – are absolutely essential for humanitarian reasons, or the peace of the world, or in the vital strategic interests of this country, but which are not endorsed in the editorials of the tabloids, will become very difficult, perhaps impossible, ever again to wage.

It means that the military – at every level, and their families – must realise that they are being committed to war not by the Queen, not by the Prime Minister, but by quite possibly very divided politicians. Service men and women may well die against the background of squabbling politicians failing to agree that what they are being sent to do is necessarily the right thing. Apart from anything else, that will have potentially dire consequences for the troops', and their families', morale.

By contrast with all of that, did not the use of the Royal Prerogative enable the Prime Minister strategically to form alliances, control timings, and position our armed forces to the best possible advantage, and to respond swiftly to attack? Militarily the Prime Minister may well have access to intelligence which justifies war, but which he nonetheless may not be able to share with Parliament and thence the potential enemy. Politically, the Royal Prerogative avoided the risk – especially when the Prime Minister commands a small parliamentary majority, or even none at all – of an otherwise perfectly legitimate and necessary military action being thwarted by pacifists or by an Opposition seeking party political advantage.

As a statesman, the Royal Prerogative enabled the Prime Minister to position himself above the political hurly-burly, and to seek to act truly in the interests of the nation as a whole. They are, after all, Her Majesty's forces, not Parliament's.

As a result of all of that, the net effect of the democratisation of war-making powers we have described is that Britain's standing in the world is very likely to be diminished. Our standing within NATO will be reduced and the strength of our strategic relationship with the US undermined. The international status of any country depends, to a significant effect, on its ability – in theory or practice – to intervene with military force. The effective removal of war-making powers from the Prime Minister under the Royal Prerogative inevitably reduces the military contribution we can make to world affairs.

The military and diplomatic consequences of the emasculation of war-making powers under the Royal Prerogative are so significant that they must not be allowed to occur unless it is done knowingly and intentionally. If it is our intention to become an inward-looking nation doing little more from a military standpoint than defending these shores, and even then doing that only in a limited way, then we must say so. If, on the other hand, we intend to remain a significant player on the world stage, a member of the UN Security Council, a nation punching above its weight in strategic terms, then we must reassess fundamentally the way in which we decide whether or not to deploy troops and engage in military activity in general. If we do not do so, we risk being relegated to the third division in international affairs; and we risk reducing the contribution we can make to the security of the world, and the security of our own people and resources.

We would be abdicating the responsibilities and international moral obligations deriving both from our imperial history and from our ranking in the top ten of the world's economies. We owe it to the world and to future generations to do our bit to preserve peace, reduce poverty and ensure security. We must now ask if we can really do that as a result of what might appear at first sight to have been a pretty minor constitutional modernisation.

4

WHAT IS WAR?

Britain, in 2014, finds herself on the horns of a constitutional, military and diplomatic dilemma. Many – as I have done in the last chapter – would argue that the continuing use by the Prime Minister of the Royal Prerogative to take the country to war has huge strategic, political and diplomatic advantages. Yet it is only right to recognise that in arguing that, I may be desperately swimming against the tide of history.

It is hard to imagine any circumstance – leaving aside dire and urgent national emergency – under which a Prime Minister could once again do as Tony Blair did in Afghanistan in 2001 and commit the country to war without any substantive debate and vote in the House of Commons. There may well be advantages in doing so, but the likelihood of it occurring, or at least occurring without a massive and probably indefensible political row, are remote in the extreme. Unfettered use by the Prime Minister of the Royal Prerogative with regard to war-making is as dead politically as the divine right of kings.

Yet it is equally true that if, indeed, Britain can never again go to war without the explicit agreement of the people through their elected representatives; if tabloid approval is to be more important than strategic intelligence; if all of that is true, then it will have pretty catastrophic consequences for our place in the world, and ultimately for world peace.

So how can we extract ourselves from this awful constitutional dilemma? Well, there just may be a way; which we will suggest later in this book.

Before putting forward our suggested solution, we must first of all be clear about what war is, if we are to find some way out of the dilemma we have described. Any new constitutional arrangement can only be effective and agreed by all if we are clear about what it is that we are being asked to consider for approval. Is it full-scale nation-on-nation war; repelling aggressors from our shores; or protecting our vital national resources? Is it humanitarian relief in faraway lands; the safe evacuation of British citizens threatened overseas; counter-insurgency, counter-piracy or counter-terrorism? Is it regime change – the promotion of democracy and free western-style liberal economics?

Just think of recent wars. Suez – the last parachute insertion at battalion strength by British troops – was a hugely controversial attempt to preserve British imperial interests; it failed, and resulted in the government falling. Malaya, Aden, Mau-Mau – all were painful rearguard actions in Britain's honourable attempt at an orderly withdrawal from empire. Korea was a Canute-like attempt to contain Communism alongside our American allies. The Cold War consumed vast amounts of taxpayers' cash, but was of course ultimately successful, with hardly a single shot needing to be fired during its fifty years or so duration. The Falklands conflict was a simple removal of an invader, as was Kuwait. The Balkans was a brave attempt to keep peace at Europe's borders and avoid a humanitarian catastrophe; Kosovo was linked and related, but unapproved by the UN Security Council. Sierra Leone, Mali, Libya were all carried out with humanitarian motives. Northern Ireland was essentially a policing operation. These conflicts have in common only their absolute differences. They all bear the loose title of 'war' and involved the aggressive deployment of military assets. Yet they have virtually nothing else in common.

Given that diversity, how is it going to be possible to try to construct some mechanism by which the nation decides either to become involved or not to do so? A decision-making mechanism which might suit one of these conflicts may be wholly inappropriate in another. A reaction to an incoming nuclear missile needs a different decision-making process to a carefully planned overseas intervention. Both bear little relationship to ongoing counter-piracy operations off Somalia, or, indeed, a daring SAS strike in Sierra Leone. The decision-making and approval processes for a skirmish on the north-west frontier will clearly be quite different to the approval and justification needed for nuclear deterrence, far less the firing of a nuclear weapon; all of which is quite different to limited deployments in defence of British civilians, and so on.

The very diversity of modern war might be thought to preclude any consistency in the processes we use to try to decide when and if to engage. Or might it actually be an argument in favour of leaving the ultimate authority not with Parliament but with the Prime Minister and government?

Or, to look at it another way, even if we cannot be too prescriptive about what modern war actually is and could be in the future, might it not be possible to agree in advance a set of parameters which render any war conducted thereafter permissible for the government of the day, as long as the pre-set conditions are satisfied? Surely we could map out those things for which the use of force is acceptable and those for which it is not.

Defending our shores against an aggressive invader is on the right of arc. Invading France to ensure a better flow of champagne would be at the opposite extreme. Between the two would be a host of justifications of a stronger or weaker persuasiveness. A dictator gassing millions of citizens is clear; one gassing only a few might be harder to justify. Terrorists planning onshore outrages are clear, freedom fighters within their own country much more marginal. The possible debates are endless.

But would it really be beyond the wit of man to hammer out a general codification of when armed intervention is possible and legal, and when it is not? And if we could agree on what is the legitimate purpose of warfare in all of its myriad formats, and crucially, if we could agree as to when and how military force could reasonably be used, might it not be possible to come to some kind of consensus about the mechanism needed for the actual deployment?

In other words, rather than asking what war is, we should be asking what war is for. If we can agree on the (comparatively) civilised purposes of military action, then the detail of the way in which it is deployed becomes much less important.

What the House of Commons needs is the ability to stipulate why our troops and military resources should be used; they do not, and should not, have a direct and detailed say in the detail of how it is to be used. So if we can create a consensual answer to the question 'Why war?' might we not be getting close to providing a solution to the question 'How should we agree to use it?'

5

WHY WAR?

The purpose and aims of wars used to be straightforward. One nation upset another; one king wanted a bit of territory; diplomats and emissaries issued demands and ultimatums. If they failed, war was declared, then waged, one side or the other won and a peace treaty was negotiated, land or money changed hands, and the course of history rolled on.

William Duke of Normandy invaded England and the Saxons tried their best to defend themselves, but lost (at least partly because the Normans understood the use of stirrups to enable the cut and thrust from horseback while the Saxons, having none, were forced to fight dismounted!), and the Normans took over England. Hitler invaded Poland, the Prime Minister's deadline passed and war was declared. It continued until the unconditional surrender of Germany six years later. The Argentinians invaded the Falklands, British forces threw them out again. Saddam Hussein invaded Kuwait and an outraged international community threw him out. A list of Britain's wars and how they were engaged will be found in the appendix to this book.

Things still seemed pretty simple when terrorists hijacked some airliners on 11 September 2001 and slammed into New York's World Trade Centre and the Pentagon in Washington DC, with a terrible loss of life and an even more dramatic effect on America's nationhood and self-respect. Their military reaction was straightforward and predictable.

Less than a month later, on 7 October 2001, American and British troops invaded Afghanistan. The justification was pretty obvious and universally agreed. Osama Bin Laden, the leader of Al Qaeda, who was self-confessedly responsible for the 9/11 outrage, was based in a cavernous hideout in the Bora Bora Mountains in southern Afghanistan. Since the Soviet withdrawal, Afghanistan had become more and more lawless, and ever more a base for international terrorism. There were terrorist training camps there.

A military reaction against Afghanistan was fair and reasonable in anyone's eyes, but it was an operation which could, and should, have been carried out with massive force in three to six months. It would, by that means, both have helped to assuage middle America's outrage, and, it was to be hoped, would also have had a dramatic effect on world terrorism, through the destruction of one of its heartlands. A powerful deterrence to others who might have similar attacks in mind. '*Pour encourager les autres*' as Voltaire would have said.

Yet, ten years later and after thousands of British, American and Afghan deaths, we are really no closer to understanding what it was that we were trying to do there than we were at the very beginning.

I remember a classic army PowerPoint presentation on our operations in Afghanistan on a visit to the troops in Helmand Province in 2007–08. Having explained what they were doing (and doing so well), the Brigadier concluded with a series of slides designed to justify the army's long-term presence in Afghanistan. A grinning farmer held up a sheaf of wheat to demonstrate our successful war against drugs (the largest opium crop of all time was nonetheless harvested in Afghanistan in 2013). The vast power generator carried at enormous price to the Kijacki Dam was the next slide – and the Brigadier cannot have known that seven or eight years later it would lie rusting where he left it – and the final slide was of two grinning schoolgirls, jotters firmly clamped under their arms on their way to school. 'And that, ladies and gentlemen,' said the Brigadier, 'is what it's all about. Security, infrastructure improvements, poppy destruction and girls' education.' I hope I was not being difficult or discourteous when I asked, 'Thank you Brigadier. Very instructive. And can you just remind me which aspect of international law allows us to deploy tens of thousands of troops in a foreign country in pursuit of better education for girls?'

'Er ... well. Um ... Good point. Isn't that a matter for you politicians?' the Brigadier mumbled.

It was quite plain then – and now – that we really had very little strategic justification for our long-term deployment in Afghanistan.

We had, if anything, even less justification for our invasion of Iraq, eighteen months after 9/11. On 20 March 2003, thousands of US and British troops crossed the bund from Kuwait into Iraq. They really had very little idea why they were doing so. Saddam, so far as we know, played no part whatsoever in 9/11. His regime was secular rather than Islamic. He had no loyalties to Osama Bin Laden nor Al Qaeda. Bin Laden and Saddam were in many ways at opposite extremes.

So why did we invade Iraq in the aftermath of 9/11? Really, no one knows. Tony Blair and his 'Dodgy Dossier' focussed on 'weapons of mass destruction' about which he claimed intelligence alleging vast quantities being ready for deployment within forty-five minutes. That he must have known this to be untrue did not deter him from using those arguments in statements to the House of Commons and elsewhere in a desperate effort to justify what he was doing.

On other occasions, Foreign Secretary Jack Straw sought to argue that it was for human rights purposes. He memorably described how prostitutes were allegedly stoned in the Baghdad streets, as if somehow or another that justified what would otherwise have been a wholly illegal war. Why, as a QC, international lawyer and Foreign Secretary, he thought that human rights violations of the kind he was describing (even if they actually occurred) justified an invasion of a sovereign territory is hard to imagine.

Why the government separately sought to justify the war with Iraq as some kind of an integral part of the otherwise reasonable 'War on Terror' is equally hard to fathom. Iraq was not part of the international terrorist networks – unlike her deadly enemy Iran. There was probably less terrorism emanating from Iraq than from almost any other Middle Eastern country, and a principal effect of the war against Saddam Hussein has been to create a brand new breeding-ground for terrorists in Iraq. Yet the invasion, and the thousands of lives subsequently lost, formed the main part of the 'War on Terror.' Why?

As I write, the Chilcot Commission, which was set up to enquire into the causes – and justifications – for the Iraq War, is singularly failing to publish its results, or to give any clue as to when it will do so.[1] There is, in particular, a debate as to whether top secret communications between Tony Blair and George Bush about the reasons behind the war may now – or ever – be published. Unless Chilcot does so, and unless he unearths evidence of genuine reasons for the invasion, the world and historians will conclude that there was no real justification for it under International Law at all. And if that is the case, Mr Blair and Mr Bush may well stand accused of a pretty heinous crime. What is clear is that no one knew, then or now, why we did as we did; why tens of thousands of lives were lost as a result; and why the West has suffered a complex of consequences from their actions.

Destroying Al Qaeda may be more or less justifiable. Protecting the West from terrorist attack seems reasonable, but regime change? Drugs? Girls' education? Hydroelectric schemes and preventing prostitutes being stoned in the streets? By no stretch of anyone's imagination could these things justify high-intensity kinetic warfare of the kind we have experienced in Iraq and Afghanistan for the last fourteen years or so.

And when UK and US troops finally leave Afghanistan at the end of 2014, will we really know whether or not the massive price paid in 'blood and treasure' will be justified? Will we have won? Will we have achieved something which future generations will recognise as having been demonstrably worth it? We shall see.

We have at our disposal today the deadliest weaponry in the history of mankind; we have the greatest ability of all time to deploy it anywhere we care to at extraordinarily short notice. Weapons and the military today have greater capacity than ever – for good or ill – around the globe, yet we really have very little idea what to do with it, or why. We are little boys blundering around the nursery playing with big boys' toys.

So surely it is time that we sat down with a cold towel around our collective heads, and worked out what warfare is and what it can legitimately be used for. If we could truly understand our military capacity in the West, and if we could discuss and codify what we believe is a legitimate use for it, we would be making credible steps towards working out a method of deciding on when and how to use these terrible capabilities.

Now some of this work is – and always has been – done by the world's military. They constantly struggle with the thinking and justification that lies behind what they do. Defence doctrine fills shelves in the library. They produce all sorts of 'Rules of Engagement' under the Geneva Convention which curtail and control the way in which we use military capabilities. NATO, the UN and national governments all have teams of civil servants struggling with the ideas; academics have produced acres of books and articles about it all. Yet despite that, we are as unclear today about why and how we go to war as we ever were. The justification and conduct of Iraq and Afghanistan were questionable in the extreme, Kosovo was conducted without UN sanction, and Vietnam was a catastrophic failure.

The civilised West really has very little idea of how and why we go to war, and that is despite several thousand years of efforts by philosophers to codify, to write down, what warfare is, what it should be, and how it can be justified. Discussion about 'the Just War' has preoccupied philosophers from the ancient Greeks, through St Thomas Aquinas, Clausewitz and up to modern times, and much modern law of conflict, from the Geneva Conventions and downwards, is based on that philosophical work.

So, in a similar way, perhaps we should now seek to codify what we as a nation and a generation believe to be 'a Just War'. We should seek to produce a broadly agreed codification of when, and why, and how, we believe it reasonable to deploy armed force around the world. If we could do that, we would be taking a major step towards working out the mechanism by which we agree to deploy that force.

Any such codification of the Just War would always have to be allowed to evolve over the generations and centuries. What was 'just' to the ancients, to medieval man, or even in the eighteenth or nineteenth centuries will almost certainly not be seen as 'just' today. Yet in any one era, surely it should be possible to produce a clearly expressed codification of what we believe the Just War should be?

An aggressive alien assaulting our shores quite plainly justifies armed self-defence with limited overseas intervention to prevent said aggressor ever reaching our shores and presumably would be acceptable to most. The defence of our interests overseas – keeping shipping lanes open and defending natural resources on which we survive is probably reasonable. Looking after British expatriates is certainly defensible, along with upholding international treaties and agreements, carrying out the will of the UN Security Council, and defending our fellow NATO states. All of these things would be widely – though inevitably not universally – accepted as being 'just'.

But what about intervening against a foreign dictator who is murdering or torturing his own people? We thought that fine against Hitler (although of course the Holocaust was never the reason for the war, since in 1939 we knew nothing about it).[2] But, Assad gassing a few hundred of his people? We were not sure. What if we knew that a mad dictator was gassing hundreds of thousands of his people – or millions? Would our decision be different then? Is it a question of quantity, or of principle? Most people appeared to feel that the interventions in Kosovo and Sierra Leone were justified by the innocent lives they saved, though others disapproved. Many people criticised the West for not intervening in Rwanda to prevent the massacre of many more innocent people, though had we done so there would certainly have been other voices raised against the use of military force.

None of these questions is easy. Yet all are capable of coherent intellectual discussion. Surely it should be possible for an intelligent society, through a process of national debate, to agree what would be fair and reasonable in terms of warfare and what would not? Surely we could produce a codified definition of the 'Just War' at any one stage in our national development, albeit that it may be necessary to amend that codification from time to time.

In other words, what I am suggesting is that we should now seek to produce a clearly expressed, nationally agreed document which lays out what we, the British people, believe is a reasonable use for our weaponry and armed forces. Doing so would prevent their improper use (Iraq, possibly Afghanistan); it would prevent their capricious or illegal use; it would permit their legitimate use (Falklands, Kuwait); and it would clarify for the troops themselves what they were doing and why.

Crucially, from the point of view of this book at least, having such a codification of what we believe to be a just war, would enable us to sort out the muddle in which our decision-making processes with regards to war find themselves post the Syria vote. If we knew plainly and openly what we would consider to be a proper use of armed force then we could presumably quite easily establish some mechanism for permitting it to happen. So let us consider the concept of the Just War and whether or not we could adapt it to our modern purposes.

6

THE JUST WAR

We have agreed in previous chapters that if the notion of 'X Factor' warfare were to become the accepted norm – if it were to be the case for all time to come that only popular wars would ever again be waged at least using British forces – then you are, at a stroke, fundamentally undermining any hope that the UK could continue to justify its international position as a leading member of the western democratic alliance, or could in any other way punch above its weight or be any kind of force for good in the world. Final abandonment of the Royal Prerogative for going to war would call into question our permanent membership of the Security Council of the UN, the firmness of NATO would be undermined, and our ability to negotiate with allies over the use of force would undeniably be curtailed.

If the tribunes of the people were to have the final say over warfare in substantive votes in the House of Commons, then how could any PM or Foreign Secretary really exercise their perfectly proper powers on the world's stage? How could they set about persuading an instinctively sceptical and pacifist electorate of the need for any war at all, no matter how convinced they themselves might be of the justification? Is there such a thing as a 'Just War', and if so, how can our statesmen set about explaining that to the electorate?

The philosophy, meaning and purpose of warfare, and the definition of the Just War have been chewed over ceaselessly by historians and philosophers since ancient times. That they

have, in that time, achieved some degree of consensus is reflected in most international law on warfare and in conventions such as those agreed in Geneva in the aftermath of the Second World War in 1949, and in several iterations since.

'*Bellum iustum*' is a form of military ethics which seeks to codify what can and cannot be done in warfare, and why. It was the ancient Indian epic *Mahabharata* which first laid down the criteria for fair or 'just' warfare, including 'proportionality' (chariots cannot attack cavalry, only other chariots, and must certainly not attack people in distress); 'just means' (no poisoned or barbed arrows); 'just cause' (no attacking out of rage) and the 'fair treatment of captives and the wounded'. Cicero built on those principles in *De Officiis*; and Saints Augustine and Aquinas codified it into medieval thinking and warfare.

St Augustine, the founder of the Church in England, was the first to declare that a Christian could be a soldier. He based his argument on Romans 13:4, 'If thou do that which is evil, be afraid; for the minister of God beareth not the sword in vain; for he is the minister of God, a revenger to execute wrath upon him that doeth evil.' That led him to argue that God had given us the sword for good reason, and that Christians could resort to violence to protect peace and punish wickedness. He even coined the phrase 'Just War', 'the wise man will wage wars ... although he would lament the necessity for it ... for if they were not just he would not wage them.' (*The City of God*)

It was 900 years later that St Thomas Aquinas used Augustine's base to codify the conditions under which a war could be 'just'. His theory of a Just War comes in three parts: *Jus ad bellum* (Justice in going to war), *Jus in bello* (Justice in making war) and *Jus post bellum* (Justice in ending a war).

Jus ad bellum has seven criteria for war:

1 Wars must be fought only on legitimate authority (although there could be a perfectly legitimate debate as to what that is and who grants it). In the Middle Ages this criterion aimed to limit conflicts by small-scale barons, captains and princelings and is often treated as the *sine qua non* of Just War theory.

2 The cause must be just. The war must be fought in order to resist aggression, protect the innocent, or to support the rights of some oppressed group. There must be significant reasons which are weighty enough to overthrow the *prima facie* duty that we should not kill or injure others. That does not include solely recapturing things taken or punishing people who have done wrong; innocent life must be in imminent danger and intervention must be to protect life.

3 The war must have the right intention. It must advance the cause of good and avoid evil, it must have clear aims and be open to negotiation; it must not be for revenge or for the sake of killing and there should be no ulterior motive. It must be waged without love of violence, or cruelty; and regret or remorse should be the proper attitude. This is shaped by the pursuit of a just cause. Since peace should be the object of war, killing is a means to that end.

4 It must be a last resort, all other attempts having failed or being unavailable.

5 There must be a reasonable hope of justice, or a reasonable chance of success in order to prevent pointless wars. If there is no such hope, then it would not just be imprudent, but there would be no good grounds to override the *prima facie* obligation not to harm others if none of the just ends can be realised, and thus going to war would be immoral.

6 There must be discrimination. Non-combatants should not be directly or intentionally attacked, although it is recognised that there may be accidental casualties.

7 There must be proportion. That is, there must be a balance between the good achieved versus the harm done. This condition takes into account the effect on all human beings, not just those on one side, and it is the effects on humans rather than any other physical damage which have priority.

Jus in bello directs how combatants are to act in war:

1 Discrimination: The acts of war should be directed towards enemy combatants. Thus prohibited acts would include bombing civilian residential areas and committing acts of terrorism or reprisal against civilians. Combatants must not attack enemies who have surrendered, have been captured, who are injured, or who do not present an immediate lethal threat.

2 Military Necessity: An attack must be intended to help in the military defeat of the enemy. It must be an attack on a military objective.

3 Proportionality. An attack must not be launched on a military objective if incidental civilian casualties would be excessive in relation to the military advantage gained.

4 Fair Treatment of prisoners of war.

5 Soldiers may not use weapons which are considered evil, such as mass rape or deforestation, or use weapons whose effects cannot be controlled, such as poison gas or carpet bombing.

Jus post bellum, (which is an element largely ignored in Iraq and Afghanistan) is almost as important. It is about the transition from conflict to peace. Its purpose is:

1 To provide assurances to combatants about the terms necessary to end a conflict.
2 To provide terms for the end of the war (once the rights of a political community have been vindicated, further continuation of the war becomes an act of aggression).
3 To provide guidelines for the construction of peace treaties.
4 To prevent, through peace negotiations, continuous fighting by belligerents trying to gain more favourable terms.
5 To prevent draconian and vengeful peace terms (the rights a 'just' state fights for in a 'just' war provide the constraints on what can be demanded from the defeated belligerent).
6 To set the terms of a just settlement for a Just War which should include:

> Elimination of unjust gains from aggression.
> Punishment against the aggressor in two forms: compensation to the victim for losses incurred, and potential war crime trials for the aggressor.
> Security for the victim against future attack by demilitarisation or political rehabilitation.
> Terms for settlement should be measured and reasonable (which rules out 'unconditional surrenders').
> Terms for settlement should be made public.
> Leaders, soldiers and civilians must be distinguished from one another.
> Civilians must be reasonably immune from punitive measures (which rules out sweeping socio-economic sanctions).

These principles of *jus ad bellum*, *in bello* and *post bellum*, first codified by Thomas Aquinas, are as old as the philosophy of warfare itself. They have been much debated and expanded and changed since Aquinas. The School of Salamanca gave examples of a Just War as being in self-defence, as long as there is a reasonable probability of success; preventing war against a tyrant who is about to attack (the law of pre-emption is still debated by international lawyers today – when would Israel be justified in a pre-emptive strike against an aggressor thought to have nuclear weapons aimed at Tel Aviv?); and to punish a guilty enemy.

The great Carl von Clausewitz (1780–1831) brought some of Aquinas' thinking slightly more up to date in his posthumously printed magnum opus, *On War*, in 1832. It removed much of the theological backing for Just War thinking, and interpreted it more in the context of the Age of Enlightenment. 'War,' he famously said, 'is the continuation of politik by other means.' 'Politik' has been variously translated as 'policy' or 'politics', which of course are very different things.

His thinking – and the dialectical way of expressing it – particularly appealed to Lenin and Marx, and later to Mao Zedong. Eisenhower adapted Clausewitz's horror of total war to justify nuclear deterrence in the 1950s. His very public nuclear tests in the Pacific were specifically designed to demonstrate the horrors of total nuclear war, thereby, he argued, avoiding it ever being used.

Clausewitz spoke only of wars between countries with well-defined armies – state armies suppressing insurgents, terrorism and asymmetric warfare, even more so remotely piloted air systems (drones), ISTAR, Special Forces and cyber warfare would, of course, have been beyond his imagination.

In more modern times, the UN have codified some of these ideas into their 'Responsibility to Protect' doctrines and operational codes. The Responsibility to Protect is a:

... Global commitment to protect populations from wide-spread and systematic atrocity crimes. The principle ... was conceived in 2001 as part of the influential International Commission on Intervention and State Sovereignty ... Individual states are reminded of their responsibility to protect their populations from four specific crimes: genocide, war crimes, ethnic cleansing and crimes against humanity. In instances where national authorities are 'manifestly failing' to protect their populations, the international community has a responsibility to take collective action.[1]

The Responsibility to Protect has three foundation 'pillars':

1 A state has a responsibility to protect its population from genocide, war crimes, crimes against humanity and ethnic cleansing.
2 The international community has a responsibility to assist the state to fulfil its primary responsibility.
3 If the state manifestly fails to protect its citizens from the four mass atrocities, and peaceful means have failed, the international community has the responsibility to intervene through coercive measures such as economic sanctions. Military intervention is considered the last resort.

Military intervention under the Responsibility to Protect was then further refined by the 2001 UN Conference. It concluded that any form of military intervention must fulfil the following six criteria:

1 Just Cause – is the threat a 'serious and irreparable harm occurring to human beings'?
2 Right Intention – is the main intention of the military action to prevent human suffering; or are there other motives?
3 Final Resort – has every other means other than military intervention been taken into account? [This does

not mean that every measure must have tried and failed, but that there are reasonable grounds to believe that only military action would work in that situation.]

4 Legitimate Authority.

5 Proportional Means – are the minimum necessary military means applied to secure human protection?

6 Reasonable Prospect – is it likely that military action will succeed in protecting human life, and are the consequences of this action certain not to be worse than no action at all?

These criteria, of course, have clear linkages back to the whole theory of the Just War as laid out, for example, by St Thomas Aquinas. They are a modern codification of an age-old philosophy, and they are proof that codification of our modern understanding of the Just War is perfectly possible.

Now it is true, of course, that there are many other – and sometimes conflicting – theories of warfare, and the justification for it. There is 'militarism', which argues that there are innate benefits to society from warfare; there is 'realism', which dismisses theories such as the Just War in favour of self-interest; revolution and civil war, which of course have no justification from a state and therefore cannot be termed 'just'; non-violent struggle; 'absolutism'; 'pacifism', which of course argues that there cannot be any such thing as a Just War; the right of self-defence, and 'consequentialism' (the end justifies the means.) These, and no doubt many more, have been developed by philosophers and thinkers and generals, sometimes to seek to justify a military course of action on which they were determined. Some are more justifiable than others.

Yet the extensive discussion about the notion of a Just War, or even the justification for warfare, by the ancients, medieval theologians and as late as Locke and Mill in the eighteenth century, and then Clausewitz in the nineteenth, rather tailed off in modern times (with one or two notable exceptions). Perhaps it is linked to a decline in religion, or even of very widespread philosophical thought. Perhaps it is a rise in pragmatism in government, or possibly it is a change in the nature of warfare itself in the last 100 years or so, that open and honest philosophical discussion among statesmen is now inhibited by popular democracy and a populist free press.

The point is that it should be possible for any given generation to sit down, chew them over and come up with an agreed codification of the justification for war. It should surely not be beyond the wit of man to create a detailed and comprehensive codification of what justifies war, how it should be conducted, how it can be avoided and how it should be ended.

Now if that can be done – if by a process of thoughtful deliberation and debate nationally, we can construct a clear and definitive view of what a Just War is and should be, what should be the reasons for it, the means by which it is to be conducted and the ways and means for its ending – if that can be done, then do we not have a sound basis for collective decision-making about war itself?

In other words, the codification of the definition of all aspects of the Just War could perhaps be the first step towards a much greater consensus and understanding of warfare, what it is, and what it can and should be used for. If that can be achieved, there may be an inherent solution here to the Royal Prerogative dilemma in which we find ourselves post 29 August 2013.

7

HOW THE AMERICANS DO IT

Before describing our proposed solution, it may be instructive to take a passing glance at the constitutional position in the United States. There are some parallels with the British conundrum, but also some stark contrasts.

In America, the President's role as commander-in-chief gives him direct power to repel attacks against the United States and makes him responsible for leading the armed forces – a role still fulfilled legally and constitutionally in the UK by the monarch herself, albeit through binding constitutional convention acting on the advice of her ministers.

However, during the Korean and Vietnam wars, the United States had found itself involved for many years in situations of intense conflict without any declaration of war or congressional approval, about which many members of Congress became increasingly concerned. Those concerns were exacerbated when news leaked out that President Nixon had conducted secret bombings of Cambodia during the Vietnam War without telling Congress. The resulting 'War Powers Resolution' which was designed to impose Congressional approval of war-making, was initially vetoed by Nixon, that veto then being overruled by a two-thirds vote in each House. The resolution finally became law on 7 November 1973.[1]

The resolution stipulates that the President can send US armed forces into action abroad only by declaration of war by Congress, 'statutory authorisation', or in case of 'a national emergency created by attack upon the United States, its territories or possessions, or its armed forces'. It requires the President to notify Congress within forty-eight hours of committing armed forces to military action, and forbids armed forces from remaining for more than sixty days, with a further thirty-day withdrawal period, without an authorisation of the use of military force or a declaration of war.

Presidents have submitted 130 reports to Congress as a result of the War Powers Resolution, although only one (the Mayaguez Incident) specifically stated that forces had been introduced into hostilities or imminent danger.

Congress invoked the War Powers Resolution in the Multinational Force in Lebanon Act,[2] which authorised the marines to remain in Lebanon for eighteen months during 1982 and 1983. In addition, the Authorization for Use of Military Force against Iraq Resolution of 1991[3] which authorised United States combat operations against Iraqi forces, stated that it constituted specific statutory authorisation within the meaning of the War Powers Resolution.

On November 9, 1993, the House used a section of the War Powers Resolution to state that US forces should be withdrawn from Somalia by March 31, 1994. In 1999, President Clinton kept the bombing campaign in Kosovo going for more than two weeks after the sixty-day deadline had passed. Even then, however, the Clinton legal team opined that its actions were consistent with the War Powers Resolution because Congress had approved a bill funding the operation, which they argued constituted implicit authorisation. That theory was controversial, because the War Powers Resolution specifically says that such funding does not constitute authorisation. Clinton's actions in Kosovo were challenged by a member of Congress as a violation of the War Powers Resolution in the DC Circuit case *Campbell* v. *Clinton*, but the court found the issue was a non-justiciable political question.

More recently, the War Powers Resolution was at issue in Bosnia, Kosovo, Iraq, and Haiti, and under President George W. Bush in responding to 9/11. In October 2002, Congress enacted the Authorization for Use of Military Force against Iraq[4] which authorised President Bush to use force as necessary to defend the United States against Iraq and enforce relevant United Nations Security Council Resolutions.

May 20, 2011, marked the sixtieth day of US combat in Libya, but the deadline arrived without President Obama seeking specific authorisation from the US Congress. Instead, he notified Congress that no authorisation was needed, since the US leadership was transferred to NATO. He was, nonetheless, rebuked for what they considered a violation of the War Powers Resolution by a vote of the US House of Representatives.

In other words, in the thirty years of its existence, the War Powers Resolution has been frequently and consistently challenged by presidents as being a possibly unconstitutional and certainly unreasonable limitation on their powers. Congress have sought to ensure its use, but the courts have failed to support them in it, so the strength of the resolution is unclear. It may be instructive that President Obama volunteered to take his Syrian strike plans to Congress after the Commons vote in August 2013. He need not, of course, have done so, since he is only obliged to consult Congress within sixty days of the start of operations. That he did so, and that he relied on David Cameron's House of Commons vote to justify it, may indicate that he was not in fact all that enthusiastic about the action in the first place. It was perhaps his 'get out of jail free' card. But his volunteering of the need for congressional approval will have weakened any subsequent attempt to restate the right of the President to act unilaterally.

That constitutional thinking on the matter in the US may be moving on may also be shown by some talk of repealing the act and replacing it with another which would be even more prescriptive of presidential powers.

On 16 January 2014, Senators John McCain and Tim Kaine unveiled legislation that would repeal the War Powers Resolution and replace it with a new law imposing a requirement for greater presidential consultation of Congress before committing military forces to war or armed conflict. Senator McCain sought to justify the idea by pointing out that Congress has not formally declared war since June 1942, since when the very nature of war has changed beyond recognition. Senator Kaine argued that modern threats require a fundamental re-examination of the relationship between a President and the legislature. The proposed replacement law would require the President to consult with Congress before deployment into a 'significant armed conflict' or engagement in combat operations expected to last more than seven days. It extends the time needed to inform Congress of the deployment to three days, but reduces the time required for a resolution to be passed by Congress for extending operations to thirty days. The proposed legislation does not affect humanitarian missions and covert operations. The proposal is based on the work of the bipartisan National War Powers Commission.

The War Powers Resolution has been controversial since it was passed. Because the Constitution limits the President's authority in the use of force without a declaration of war by Congress, there is controversy as to whether the provisions of the resolution are consistent with the Constitution. Presidents have therefore drafted reports to Congress to state that they are 'consistent with' the War Powers Resolution rather than 'pursuant to' so as to take into account the presidential position that the resolution is unconstitutional.

So at first glance it appears that there is a direct and clear contrast between the UK and US. Unlike America, where the President receives a mandate from Congress albeit often after the event, in the UK the Prime Minister could until now have acted unilaterally using the ancient Royal Prerogative.

The reality, however, may be less stark. There is a delicacy in the British Constitution, which, while unwritten, is nonetheless very much a reality. One of the great advantages of the UK Constitution is that it is 'living and breathing'.

It constantly changes, both in reaction to structural amendments, such as the Bill of Rights, The Act of Settlement, the Act of Union, the Parliament Acts, the establishment of the Scottish Parliament and the Welsh Assembly and the partial abolition of the hereditary peerage, and in reaction to sometimes almost unseen changes to parliamentary practice and procedure. The flexibility of the unwritten British constitution stands in stark contrast to the inflexibility of the written American constitution – which was thought by the Founding Fathers to be the best way of curbing the over-mighty powers of the Executive. There may be a lesson here for those seeking to curb the use of the Royal Prerogative by Act of Parliament.

So whereas in America there was almost no substantive discussion in Congress prior to the war in Iraq because the view of the President was deemed sufficient, in Britain if a Prime Minister were to seek to take the country to war without keeping Parliament informed, and without MPs' at least tacit consent, his position would quickly become untenable. The Royal Prerogative cannot be represented as any sort of personal uninhibited mandate. As we hope our short historical tour in chapters 9, 10 and 11 will show, it was never so even in the hands of medieval kings and certainly is not so in the hands of a modern Prime Minister.

For the reality is that the Prime Minister acts within the complex web which is the British Constitution, and which includes Crown, Lords, Commons, Executive, Civil Service, judiciary, even the political parties. He knows that ignoring any part of it would unbalance the rest. A Prime Minister considering committing the country to war needs to secure the support of the people at large, and of their representatives in Parliament. If he does not have it, then it is likely to lead to failure of his own support and ultimately of a Vote of No Confidence and a quick general election. It is not 'Prime Ministerial Prerogative' which allows him to commit troops to war, it is the 'Royal Prerogative' which he has the power to exercise only as long as he commands a majority in the House of Commons.

8

THE ROYAL PREROGATIVE, DEMOCRACY AND THE JUST WAR

The unfettered use of the Royal Prerogative to go to war is no longer politically acceptable, even if there may well be strong arguments in its favour. The notion that the Prime Minister and Cabinet take us to war based on powers inherited from over-mighty medieval monarchs without further reference to the House of Commons is, from now on, wholly unacceptable. But the strategic and diplomatic consequences of taking every military decision to the floor of the House of Commons equally has extraordinarily serious consequences for our ability to project power for the good of the nation and of the world, as is our moral and historic duty.

The Royal Prerogative may have outlived its political usefulness, but X Factor decision-making by backbench MPs is impossible unless we are to retreat from the world altogether. So what are we to do about it? What is the answer to the Royal Prerogative dilemma?

We suggest that there might be a solution inherent in the codification of the Just War which we have proposed.

What we are proposing is that an agreed codification of the Just War should be written into statute. There would have to be a very extensive period of public and political debate about it, and then, assuming that some degree of consensus could be achieved about the definition and parameters of a Just War, it would come before Parliament like any other bill. It would be proposed by ministers in the usual way (although since it involves a change to the Royal Prerogative it would, I think, technically require the Queen's consent, very unusually, prior to second reading rather than at the end of all parliamentary procedures, as would be more normal). It would be considered by both Houses in exactly the same way as any other bill, and assuming that it completed its passage would be signed off by the monarch.

At the end of all of that, we would have on the statute book an Act laying out the pre-conditions under which in any given situation we can deploy armed force, the way in which the military action would be carried out, and indeed the way in which it would be brought to a completion. The Prime Minister and government would then be free to act as they thought best – and without any further vote in either House – as long as they remain within the statutory pre-conditions laid down in the enabling Act. The legal sanction for any failure to abide by the terms of the statute would then be clear. If they did not do so, they would as usual be liable to judicial review, or possibly (if appropriate in the light of the immediate military situation) injunction to prevent them acting outside or against the law. In fact,

Is there a way of defining responsibilities and powers amongst Cabinet, Parliament, and the public when war is envisaged? Perhaps there is.

they would be subject to precisely the same parliamentary and political constraints and sanctions as they are now on every occasion that they exercise any power granted them by statute.

In other words, under this scenario, Prime Ministers would be able to behave in very much the way they used to under the powers conferred upon them by the Royal Prerogative, but the things which they would be allowed to do, or not do, would be laid down, not in practice and custom, and certainly not by delegation from the monarch, but in the law of the land. Crucially, those powers would therefore have been granted to the Prime Minister not by the monarch, but by Parliament itself. Parliament would have asserted its right to decide in advance the reasons for, and conduct of, a war without hampering the actual conduct of it.

It has been pointed out to me that there is a (perhaps marginal) risk that if we were publicly to codify our war-making intentions in this way, any potential enemy would always be tempted to 'test them to their limits'. In other words, they would go as far as they thought they could go while still avoiding armed intervention by the UK. That, of course, is exactly the position at the moment, and therefore must be a relatively minor risk which, in my view, does not undermine the proposal.

This solution avoids all of the complications and hindrances inherent in the X Factor approach to war without seeking to preserve the unpreservable – namely war-making powers under the Royal Prerogative.

Without wishing further to complicate the proposed Act, it might also be worth incorporating into it a further codification proposed most recently in a paper produced by historian James de Waal. His seminal paper on 'British Political–Military Relations 2001–10'[1] argues very convincingly that the whole structure of political/military relations in the UK is haphazard and muddled and relies on 'trusting the right people' rather than any more formal rules about how the military and political people need to interact:

> Taking the Iraq and Afghanistan examples, a picture emerges of a policy process in which there is:
>> A perception of lobbying by elements of the armed forces to support their institutional interests.
>> A consequent lack of political confidence in military advice.
>> A lack of clarity over which issues fall within the competence of military advisers and commanders, and which remain outside.
>> A disconnect between the deployment of military force and the political aims it is supposed to serve.
>> Considerable confusion over how some critical and far-reaching decisions were actually taken.

He concludes:

> The government should make its decision-making process on the use of force subject to a formal code, approved by Parliament. This code should define the process through which decisions are taken, and the roles and responsibilities of those involved. It would help preserve the political impartiality of the armed forces, underscoring that their advice must be based on their professional military assessment. It would also aid accountability by showing who gave what advice, when and why. And the code would improve the quality of decisions by providing a firm framework upon which policy-makers could rely when under pressure.

Such a codification might well prove useful in the aftermath of the formal conclusions of the enquiry by Sir John Chilcot into political/military decision-making in the run-up to the Iraq War. Even short of the final conclusions, whose publication has, at the time of writing, been delayed,[2] the publicly available evidence provided to Chilcot is, as de Waal says, 'unparalleled in quantity, scope, detail and confidentiality', and 'gives an extraordinary insight into the business of government at the time when decisions were made'.

Such a code as Mr de Waal proposes would be an adjunct to, rather than an alternative to a 'Just War Code' of the kind we are proposing. But it might well prove timely to set about legislating for them both together.

In a similar way, a recent Policy Exchange leaflet by Thomas Tugendhat and Laura Croft[3] discusses the way in which human rights legislation, in particular, undermines the ability of the British to wage war using many of the traditional methods and tactics. Their conclusion offers seven options for action by the government to countermand this malign influence, under which, as they say 'British troops are being defeated not by the enemy but by our own lawyers'. Several of them call for legislation to exempt the MOD from corporate manslaughter, and to derogate from the European Convention on Human Rights during deployed operations and in a number of other ways. Their suggestions could reasonably form a part of the same Act.

Such an Act would help to absolve any Prime Minister from any risk of prosecution by the International Criminal Court if he were to have taken the country to a war which the international community had not recognised as being 'just'. Having the allowable reasons for war codified in statute in the way we have proposed would put him in very much the same position as the President of the United States with any such potential liability at least very much reduced, very probably to vanishing point.

Writing the principles of the *Bellum Iustum* into law, and then allowing the Prime Minister to act within the terms of that law seems to us a neat and simple solution to what could otherwise become a massive hindrance on Britain's ability to act for the good of the world. We very much hope that academics and think tanks, government officials and constitutionalists will pay serious attention to it; and that it may form a part of the manifesto of both main political parties.

We want the Prime Minister to take us to war not using the 'Royal Prerogative', but using a new 'Parliamentary Prerogative'.

PART THREE: WHO USED TO TAKE BRITAIN TO WAR?

BY MARK LOMAS QC

EDWARD III.

Edward III (1327–1377). The expense of waging war saw a fundamental shift of power from the sovereign to Parliament during his reign.

DIVINE RIGHT OF KINGS?

Early Origins of the Royal Prerogative

If we are to understand the constitutional implications of the momentous and historic shambles played out on the floor of the House of Commons on the evening of 29 August 2013 we need to understand how the Royal Prerogative to take the country to war was established and adapted over 1,000 years of English history. We need to find out how the Royal Prerogative arose, exactly what it was, how it has evolved over the centuries and how an essentially medieval royal power of awesome dimensions came to survive the development of parliamentary democracy and to be exercised in the Queen's name by prime ministers and cabinets into the twenty-first century.

A fundamental power of the King has, from the earliest times, been the power to go to war with his enemies and to command his subjects to go with him. The King would see it as his right, and his subjects would see it as their duty. But in practice there have always been limits to the exercise of that right, and checks and balances on that theoretically absolute power. For example, before the unification of England under Alfred the Great and the Wessex-based Anglo-Saxon and Danish kings that followed him, the ambit of the King's power was uncertain. He commanded obedience from his immediate tribal or geographic followers and neighbours but beyond them he could not be certain who would answer any summons to arms. That would depend on his reputation and power, on local interests and probably on precisely who was the enemy.

Later, customary limits were developed. The King, and each of the principal earls, commanded standing forces of professional, trained soldiers – housecarls owing personal loyalty to their lord alone – their numbers depending on the status and wealth of the earl in question. They were elite troops and formed the core of any Anglo-Saxon army. Assuming the earl commanding them was loyal, their attendance on the summons could be relied upon. Beyond them the bulk of the army would be composed of the fyrd, a territorial body of armed peasants commanded by their local thegn. For the fyrd, custom placed a limit on the Royal Prerogative. They could be summoned to muster, usually through the local shire-moot, and required to attend, but only for a fixed number of days. After that, they were free to return to their fields. That became a critical issue in the autumn of 1066, when the army, mustered to blockade the south coast against a Norman landing, needed to disperse for the harvest. It may well have been one reason why William delayed his invasion for so long.

After the Conquest, the old Anglo-Saxon tradition of purely personal service was replaced by the Norman feudal system, where landowners held their land as tenants either of superior lords or of the King, and each tenancy carried with it an obligation to fight for one's lord when summoned and to provide a set number of men-at-arms in response to a call to muster. In this can be seen the origin of the Royal Prerogative: a duty to fight in return for the privilege of holding property from the Crown. However, in practice, even then the power to command the feudal levy to muster and go to war was neither arbitrary nor absolute. The difficulties experienced by Edward I and his war in Gascony, described in the next section, will illustrate the point.

The Maintenance of the Prerogative After the Emergence of Parliament

Parliament, in the sense of a legislative and deliberative body made up of two parts – lords spiritual and temporal in one, and commoners in the other – emerged in dimly recognisable form during the reign of Henry III, following the de Montfort rebellion in 1263, and was developed by slow degrees thereafter.

Edward I (Henry's son) was the first to make regular use of Parliament, primarily for money-raising purposes to fund his wars of conquest against the Welsh and the Scots, and to defend his feudal possessions in Gascony against the French crown. The Celtic campaigns were a serious drain on the resources of the kingdom and heavy taxes were required to fund them. When Edward was finally able to turn his attention to France, he called a Parliament to meet in Salisbury in February 1297 in order to seek funds for a new campaign, stating in his writ of summons: 'What touches all should be approved by all.' However (with a faint echo of 2013), the country was thoroughly war-weary. Taxes levied for earlier campaigns had been particularly severe. The tax on wool (the so-called '*maltote*', or 'bad toll') had driven down the price paid by merchants to farmers, causing a general recession. The clergy, hiding behind a new Archbishop and a Papal Bull condemning royal levies on the church, refused further financial assistance, causing Edward to commission royal officers to seize church property.

The whole thing came to a head at the Parliament in Salisbury. Edward's plan of campaign against the French was to divide his forces, leading one half himself through Flanders from the north and sending the other half directly to Gascony to relieve the local forces and attack the French from the south. The barons deputed to make up the southern force refused en masse to go. The point they stood on was a legal one. They asserted that their feudal duty required them to fight with the King, but it did not give him the right to demand that they go to fight in a foreign land without him. Their leader, the Earl of Norfolk and Marshall of England, is reported by a contemporary chronicler to have argued:

'With you will I gladly go, O King, in front of you in the first line of battle as belongs to me by hereditary right', he said.

'You will go without me too, with the others', Edward replied.

'I am not bound, neither is it my will, O King, to march without you', said the Earl.

Enraged the King burst out, so it is said, with these words: 'By God, O Earl, either you will go or you will hang!'

'By the same oath', replied Norfolk, 'I will neither go nor hang'.[2]

In the event the Earl did neither. Edward pressed ahead with his plans, impounding clerical property and calling in debts owed by magnates. Some of the clergy and leading nobles, including Norfolk and the Earl of Hereford, Constable of England, continued to dig in their heels and refuse to take their forces to Gascony. Parliament broke up in Salisbury in March 1297 without any decision and was recalled to Westminster in July. By then Edward had made peace with the Archbishop of Canterbury and pleaded his case with the common people assembled in Westminster, acknowledging mistakes had been made and offering a reissue of Magna Carta. The earls continued to resist, drawing up a list of 'remonstrances'. In August, Edward ordered a further series of heavy taxes on the church, a general levy of one-eighth of moveable property and a seizure of wool. He claimed these measures had been justified 'in Parliament'. His opponents dismissed his so-called 'Parliament' as simply 'the people stood about in his chamber' and the earls broke into the Exchequer and forbade the collection of wool or of the eighth.[3] This was a total stand-off.

In the face of it Edward simply sailed for Flanders with the forces he could command and began the northern arm of his invasion of France. The forces intended for the planned southern arm, to be led by the rebellious earls, simply never sailed. The campaign proved a disaster and ended with a hastily cobbled together two-year peace treaty. And there the matter rested. It was overtaken by a renewed revolt in Scotland, led by William Wallace. In the face of that threat to English interests, the country reunited, Edward called a new Parliament in May 1298, further concessions were made, the '*maltote*' was abolished, and sufficient funds were produced to meet the Scottish threat.

So what conclusions can be drawn from these events, about the scope of the Royal Prerogative at the very outset of the development of Parliament in a form we can begin to recognise?

First, it is clear that the Prerogative was no more unfettered or absolute than it had been before the Conquest. As with the Saxon Earls and the fyrd, there were limits to the obligations of the nobles required to provide the men and do the fighting. Second, the King's ability to go to war was at least circumscribed in the absence of parliamentary support, because of the difficulties of supply. Wars are expensive and the King needed support in Parliament to ensure the necessary taxes could be levied.

Neither of these constraints, of course, directly impinge on the King's absolute right to make a declaration of war itself – the central concern of this book. No one suggested that Edward I did not have the right to declare war on the King of France. The constraint was on the question of the ability of the King – of the Crown – successfully to prosecute a war once it had been declared. That critical distinction is one that, on the whole, and with some hiccoughs, was maintained throughout the succeeding 715 odd years – at least until 29 August 2013.

The next serious foreign war to involve England
resulted from Edward III's assertion of his right to the
throne of France. There was no question of putting the
issue before Parliament before asserting his claim (which
was, genealogically speaking, better than King Philip's).
In 1337 he swore an oath (in the words of an apocryphal
contemporary ballad):

> I will defy the king of St. Denis. And I will cross the
> sea, my subjects with me ... I will set the country ablaze
> and there I will await my mortal enemy, Philip of Valois,
> who wears the fleur-de-lis ... If he and his subjects attack
> me, I will fight him, he can be sure of that, even if I have
> only one man to his ten. Does he believe that he can
> take my land from me? If I once paid him homage ...
> I renounce him, you can be sure of that, for I will make
> war on him by word and deed. With my oath I have
> undertaken this vow.[4]

In due course he departed for Flanders to link up with his
allies, and made a public declaration of his claim before a
large crowd in the market square in Ghent. There he displayed for the first time the new royal Coat of Arms, with the
lions of England quartered with the fleurs-de-lis of France.

It is clear that Parliament had no say in any of these symbolic but momentous events, encompassing the declaration
of what developed into the Hundred Years' War. However,
just as in the days of his grandfather, Parliament had an
increasing amount to say about Edward's prosecution
of the war. Despite the initial crushing victory in the sea
battle at Sluys in 1340, the war proved inconclusive and,
as usual, ruinously expensive. Edward ran up eye-watering
levels of debt to his Flemish and German allies and to the
Italian banking houses, to whom at one point he pawned
the crown jewels, and the administration left behind in
England became increasingly unwilling to continue to fund
the adventure.

Eventually there was a serious showdown. Edward reappeared unannounced in England, sacked his Chancellor and Treasurer, had two senior judges, the Constable of the Tower and several leading merchants arrested, bypassed the clerks at the exchequer and ordered tax receipts to be paid directly into an emergency treasury at the Tower of London. Then he turned on the head of the Regency Council, the Archbishop of Canterbury. But he had finally overreached himself. A Parliament was called in March 1341. Edward tried to exclude the Archbishop from the Painted Chamber and allowed in several of his people who had no right to be there. The leading earls protested, the interlopers were ejected and the Archbishop admitted – to be presented by the King with a list of thirty-two charges of misconduct.

During the days of debate that followed the whole weight of national support swung behind the Archbishop, including the great magnates, the leading prelates, the merchant community of London and – significantly – the Parliamentary Commons. In the face of such united opposition Edward had no option but to climb down. Through the mediation of the leading earls he agreed to a momentous programme of parliamentary reform that started the long process of permanently altering the balance between King and Parliament. Most significantly, tax collectors were made directly accountable to Parliament; the great ministers of state – the Chancellor, the Treasurer, the Keeper of the Privy Seal, the judges and the leading officers of the royal household – were to be sworn into office in Parliament; and lords and royal ministers were to be immune from arrest or trial 'except in Parliament and by their peers'[5] – the birth of the concept of 'parliamentary privilege'.

So the price for Edward III of a reliable flow of funds to support his war with France was a permanent recognition of the power of Parliament – including, for the first time, a defined and separate body of parliamentary Commons. His pressing need for war finance had, inadvertently, brought about constitutional changes with momentous implications for the prosecution of the war with France (and any future war) and for the future governance of the kingdom. Henceforth, Parliament, including the Commons, would have scrutiny of the system of tax collection and of the exercise of power by the leading officers of the Crown – powers that gave it a large measure of control over the conduct of war.

The dividends for Edward were immediate. Instead of the previous ad hoc system of levies on moveables, forced loans and compulsory purveyance, Parliament voted him a direct tax on wool – England's chief export and source of wealth – that yielded an enormous and regular revenue (commemorated to this day by the 'Wool Sack' on which the Lord Speaker sits in the House of Lords.) Thereafter, England was able to keep its initially highly successful army continuously supplied and in the field, even during the appalling economic dislocation caused by the Black Death that laid its hand across Europe in 1348 and the decades that followed. As a result, England, led by Edward III and heavily reliant on its revolutionary weapon of mass destruction, the longbow, won a historic victory at Crécy against impossible odds in 1346; captured Calais in 1347 and turned it into an English town; and captured and held to ransom the King of France in another crushing victory at Poitiers against even more impossible odds in 1356, this time led by Edward's son, the seemingly invincible Black Prince.

The pattern first discernible during Edward I's reign was being repeated and reinforced during that of his grandson. The declaration of war remained firmly within the Royal Prerogative. The financing of the war thereafter moved increasingly into the power of Parliament, which after 1341 was much more recognisably in the modern format of separate Lords and Commons. The latter were still very much in the shadow of the former but becoming increasingly conscious of their power. That was made starkly apparent by the 1370s, with the King in his dotage, the Black Prince mortally sick, the war leaderless and going badly, and the power vacuum filled by corrupt royal hangers-on. In the so-called 'Good Parliament' of 1376 the Commons stepped out of the shadows of the Lords and firmly asserted themselves. They elected a Speaker, Walter de la Mare, and swore oaths of mutual support for each other. They then refused to grant any taxation for the continuance of the war until the corrupt ministers of the Crown had been prosecuted and removed. Various ministers were brought to trial before Parliament and, when the Speaker was asked who brought the charges against them, he replied that they did so 'in common'.

It would still not have occurred to any medieval parliamentarian, however radical, to question the Royal Prerogative to declare war independently of Parliament. But it was increasingly clear that no King of England could thereafter hope to prosecute a war successfully without the active consent and support of Parliament.

The important precedents established by Edward III and his parliaments were followed closely by Henry V when, early in the fifteenth century, he renewed the Plantagenet claim to the crown of France. The declaration of war, raised into legend by Shakespeare in his scene with the Dauphin's tennis balls in Westminster Hall, was delivered through heralds in traditional style, and the necessary supply duly voted by an enthusiastic parliament and clergy – in Shakespeare's words: '... never king of England Had nobles richer and more loyal subjects, Whose hearts have left their bodies here in England And lie pavilion'd in the fields of France.'[6]

The Balance of Prerogative and Parliament Under the Tudors

The pattern that emerged in the Middle Ages held good for the next 200 years, though for much of the period England was too bound up with the dynastic power struggle between York and Lancaster to have time for foreign adventures.

Elizabeth I at her most regal. Gone are the plain 'Protestant' garments she wore during Mary's reign. By guile, thrift and sheer force of personality she was able to control her parliaments to quite an extraordinary degree. But when war threatened, funds could only be raised when Parliament sat.

The end of the Wars of the Roses and the emergence of the Tudors saw a reduction in the feudal power of the great landed families and a considerable centralisation of power and administration. In particular, supply was put on a more regular basis, with Parliament being required, at least in normal times, simply to pass a 'Bill of Subsidy'. The long, slow struggle by Parliament to enlarge the scope of its rights at the expense of the Royal Prerogative and to grope its way towards the concept of popular sovereignty that we now understand continued throughout the period, but in muted form until the death of Elizabeth I in 1603.

The key instrument of administration throughout Elizabeth's reign was the Privy Council, developed under her father and grandfather. It consisted of twenty or so men of experience, comprising the principal ministers of state and officials of the royal household. They were individually chosen and appointed by the Queen and they advised her on all matters of policy, domestic and foreign, and conducted all the day-to-day business of the state in her name. It is tempting to draw parallels between the Council and today's Cabinet on the basis that the two bodies perform similar executive functions, but the critical difference is that Elizabeth II's Cabinet is responsible to Parliament whereas Elizabeth I's Council was responsible solely to the Queen.

Government under Elizabeth I was carried on principally under Royal Prerogative, and Parliament enjoyed a severely restricted sphere of competence. The Queen in Council could modify the law simply by proclamation (as it still can in strictly defined circumstances) and, thanks to her frugality, the monarch was in large part financially independent of Parliament. All 'ordinary' revenue was under her direct control and derived from sources beyond parliamentary control, once the original subsidy had been voted into law. She therefore relied on Parliament only for 'extraordinary' revenue, required in extraordinary times. She had, and exercised, the power to call parliaments and to prorogue or dismiss them at will, and it is notable that, during her forty-five years on the throne, parliaments were in session and actually sitting for a total of only thirty-five months. All in all, despite her famed ability to charm, cajole or bully Parliament into giving her what she wanted, she had a pretty old-fashioned view of the relationship, responding on one occasion to a delegation from Parliament who had the temerity to try to tell her what she should do: 'It is mon-strous that the feet should direct the head.'[7]

Inevitably, extraordinary times duly arrived with the threat from Spain and the forces of Catholic Europe, and Elizabeth was now obliged to turn, grudgingly, to Parliament for assistance. The intensification of the war with Spain and increasing commitments in France and the Spanish Netherlands required Elizabeth to summon Parliament for the express purpose of providing 'treasure' for military and naval purposes. Grants were made by Parliament on the express proviso that they were not to be treated as 'precedents' (which the Queen naturally thereaf-ter treated them as), and an issue of privilege arose between the Lords and Commons, the House of Commons asserting that it had the sole right to determine the level of any grant of finance (a constitutional battle not finally won until the passing of the Parliament Act 1911, after the House of Lords vetoed Lloyd George's 'People's Budget' of 1909).

However, on the issue of going to war, the pattern set during the Middle Ages without question held good. No Elizabethan parliamentarian, however radical (and some were sufficiently outspoken to earn themselves spells in the Tower), would have dared to suggest they had any right to question or curtail the decisions and actions of the Queen in Council in the sphere of foreign relations, diplomacy, alliance – or war.

Limited Pre-emptive Military Action – Then and Now

A tentative parallel between the reigns of the two Elizabeths can be drawn that is directly relevant to the Syrian debate described in chapter 1 and to the subject matter of this book.

In early 1587, intelligence reached the Privy Council that the King of Spain was assembling ships and war materiel in Cadiz for the purpose of sending an Armada to support the invasion of England by the Duke of Palma's forces in the Netherlands. In early 2013, intelligence reached the Cabinet that Assad's forces in Syria were using chemical weapons against the rebels. Both took the strategic decision that limited pre-emptive military action was required and justified.

In April 1587 the Queen in Council ordered Sir Francis Drake to take a force of ships and 'to impeach the purpose of the Spanish fleet ... [by whatever means, including] distressing their ships within their havens'.[8] The force immediately sailed and (nimbly eluding the Queen's countermanding order) duly carried out the Council's command and burned part of the Spanish fleet and its supplies in Cadiz Harbour. In August 2013 the Prime Minister in Cabinet, having assembled his forces in Cyprus and elsewhere and informed the world and our major ally that he intended to order military strikes against Syria, decided to put the matter to a vote in Parliament. The House of Commons failed to pass the required (or any) motion, and consequently no force sailed.

The proposition that Parliament had a right of veto over any executive decision to take military steps considered necessary in the defence of national interests – whether aggressively in ordering Drake to Spain in 1587 or defensively in ordering the home fleet to confront the Armada in home waters in 1588 – would have been met with blank astonishment by any subject of Elizabeth I. The same proposition in August 2013 was met with similar astonishment by some subjects of Elizabeth II, but with relief by others. It is therefore worth considering just what has changed between the two Elizabethan periods.

The remainder of the story, until August 2013, is the story of the slow, uneven but steady process by which the executive arm of government shifted from the Queen in Council to the Queen in Parliament, but of the survival of the Royal Prerogative despite it.

The Stuart Succession – King and Parliament Test the Boundaries

The arrival of James I from Scotland put an end to the broad consensus of the Elizabethan years, and Parliament started to flex its muscles with renewed vigour. James was determined to pursue a pro-Spanish policy – including a proposed marriage between his son Charles (later Charles I) and a Spanish princess – that ran directly counter to the feelings of the English Protestant majority who still saw Spain as their natural enemy.

An English army was raised and deployed in the Palatinate, in order to help James' son-in-law, the Elector Palatine, regain his lands, and James was obliged to summon a parliament to vote the necessary supply. The Commons demanded that first they should be told against precisely what enemy it was intended to deploy the army, and expanded their concerns into a petition about the direction of foreign policy, the Spanish marriage and the religious and political situation in Europe generally. James wrote to the Speaker of the House of Commons rebuking him for allowing debate on matters well beyond the House's remit and tending to violate the Royal Prerogative, and asserted his right to punish 'misdemeanours in Parliament'.[9]

This led to the Commons producing a 'Protestation' on 18 December 1621 in which they asserted 'that the liberties, franchises, privileges and jurisdictions of Parliament are the ancient and undoubted birthright and inheritance of the subjects of England; and that the arduous and urgent affairs concerning the King, state, and the defence of the realm ... are proper subjects and matter of counsel and debate in parliament'.[10]

That passage is of obvious significance to our topic. The Protestation went on to assert 'that every such member of the said house hath like freedom from all impeachment, imprisonment, and molestation (other than by the censure of the house itself) ...' – an assertion of parliamentary privilege at

the heart of the dispute that continued to grow during James'
reign and led in the end to the outbreak of civil war and the
eventual beheading of James' son, Charles I, in 1649.

James I's reaction was predictable: he simply prorogued,
and finally dissolved, Parliament – a key weapon in the
monarch's armoury, much used by his predecessor and not
finally resolved until after the Glorious Revolution in 1688.
However, he had underestimated the strength of feeling in
the country, as reflected in the House of Commons, against
his pro-Spanish policy. After three years and the failure of his
negotiations with Spain he executed an astonishing U-turn.
He summoned a new Parliament and in February 1624, in
his speech from the throne at the opening, undertook to
give Parliament full details of his negotiations and promised: 'I shall then entreat your good and sound advice ...'[11]
Thereafter he abandoned his long-pursued policy, followed
the wishes of Parliament and united the country against
Spain. He died shortly afterwards in 1625 leaving the country effectively at war with Spain, though there is no record
of any formal declaration of war either by him or Charles I.

This may be said to be the first, and is possibly the only,
time a war has been started at the express wish of Parliament
and contrary to the wishes of the monarch. However that
may be, what was quite clear was that Parliament was no
longer prepared to occupy the subordinate position that
it had had to accept under the Tudors, though the nature
and ambit of its new role remained to be worked out, and
would not be so until after the Hanoverian succession
under James I's great-grandson, George I.

In the meantime, James' son Charles I's solution to the
conundrum was simply to rule, as far as he could, without Parliament at all. His father had developed sources
of funds – impositions, levies on merchandise, customs
dues and so on – that were almost sufficient to meet
the ordinary needs of the Crown at least in peacetime.
Charles developed those, including the imposition of ton-
nage and poundage, the sale of monopolies, the revival

of the ancient right of 'Distraint of Knighthood' and the expansion countrywide in peacetime of the notorious 'ship money' (customarily a tax levied only in wartime and only from coastal towns to pay for naval defence). Despite growing unpopularity with the tax-paying classes – essentially the merchant and landowning communities – he managed to get along pretty well without summoning any parliaments whatsoever for nearly twelve years, from 1629 to 1640. The price of doing so was to stay out of any military commitments of any kind. He therefore made peace with Spain and France, and resisted all pressure from the Protestant majority in the country to get involved in the Thirty Years' War of religion raging on the Continent and go to the assistance of his brother-in-law, the Elector Palatine, who was embattled by the Catholic forces of the Emperor. He knew that, were he to do so, he would immediately be obliged to call a Parliament to grant the necessary supply, and then the long-dammed tide of resentment and protest would break over him.

Eventually, and fatally, Charles was sucked into war with his own northern kingdom, Scotland, over the attempted imposition of the Anglican prayer book. He raised an army without recalling Parliament and marched north. Very soon the financial position became impossible to sustain and, after trying without success to negotiate a deal with the Scottish Covenanters, he was forced to call a parliamentary election in March 1640 – his first for over eleven years. The Court party fared predictably badly in the election, the so-called Short Parliament proved impossible to control and, despite an offer to grant a lump sum of £650,000 in return for the abolition of ship money, Charles (giving an early display of his celebrated inability to recognise a good deal when he saw one, that finally cost him his head) dissolved Parliament in May.

Very soon, financial necessity caused by rising military expenses forced him to seek further supply and, in a last-ditch attempt to avoid summoning another Parliament, he resorted to the desperate expedient of calling a Great Council of Peers. When asked how they advised he should raise the finance needed to keep his army against the Scots in the field, the peers simply responded by suggesting he make peace with the Scots. Eventually he was forced to bow to the inevitable and called a fresh election.

The so-called 'Long Parliament' was elected, and sat for the first time on 3 November 1640. It was implacably opposed to what it called the King's 'arbitrary and tyrannical government against law'.[12] To prevent itself simply being dissolved again and not recalled – the usual fate of disobliging parliaments – it first passed the Triennial Act, requiring Parliament to be recalled at least once every three years (and providing for the Lord Keeper and twelve peers to summon a new Parliament if the King failed to do so). Then it passed an Act which provided that it could only be dissolved at all by the agreement of its own members – an act of collective tyranny equivalent in its own way to the King's previous power to dissolve it at will and not recall it.

The Long Parliament would not finally be dissolved until 16 March 1660, by which time it had impeached and forced the execution without trial of the King's principal minister of state, the Earl of Strafford; declared itself irremovable; gone to war with the forces of the Crown; raised a New Model Army and subordinated itself to it; and finally tried and beheaded the King himself, their lawfully constituted head of state. This taught England a valuable but hard-learned lesson that the French were to learn in 1792 and the Russians in 1918, and that England's present parliamentarians, pressing for the total abolition of the Royal Prerogative, would do well to remember today: that an elected body, freed from the constraints of constitutional limits to its power, can and will act just as tyrannically as a head of state freed from the same constraints.

These events represent dramatic proof of the advancing power and ambition of Parliament and of the fact that a King could no longer hope successfully to rule the country, much less carry on a war, without the support of and supply from a duly elected Parliament. They did not, however, following the restoration of the monarchy in 1660, have any permanent constitutional effect whatsoever on the survival of the Royal Prerogative to take the country to war. That had to wait for another twenty-eight years and a further constitutional crisis.

1688 – Glorious Revolution: Parliament Dictates the Terms

Despite the prolonged and bloody upheaval it caused, the Civil War between Charles I and Parliament resolved nothing final from a constitutional point of view, because with the Restoration came, at least in theory, a reversion to the status quo ante. Charles II had been King *de jure*

William of Orange (1650–1702) is invited onto English soil by Protestant notables in 1688. He and his wife, Mary Stuart, were jointly offered the Crown by parliament in 1689.

from the moment his father's head was parted from its body. All that was required was a short Act of Parliament confirming that all proceedings of the usurping government were a nullity,[13] followed by a special Act confirming decisions of the courts between 1649 and 1660, subject to specified exceptions.[14]

So if one is looking for any real constitutional change to the scope or operation of the Royal Prerogative, one has to look for it in the expulsion of James II in 1688, and the constitutional settlement known as the 'Glorious Revolution' that followed it.

The revolutionary aspect of the settlement started with the manner of accession of the new King, William III (then Prince of Orange) jointly with his wife, Mary II, eldest daughter of James II by his first wife. After James' departure an election was held and a 'Convention' (not technically a Parliament, in the absence of a royal summons) assembled. By a small majority in the Commons and a very small majority in the Lords, James II's crown was declared forfeit so that the throne was vacant – in itself a unique and unprecedented constitutional position. Then the 'Declaration of Rights' was drawn up, setting out various restrictions to the Royal Prerogative as conditions for the offer of the crown to the prospective new monarchs. Finally, after considerable debate, the Crown was formally offered by both houses of Parliament to William and Mary jointly and the Declaration was signed into law in 1689 as the Bill of Rights.

The settlement of 1689 was a pragmatic solution that sufficed to put the new regime in place. It was clear that the balance between Crown and Parliament had permanently shifted, and an irrevocable step had been taken on the long march from the powers of the Crown being exercised by the Monarch in Council to the same powers being exercised by Cabinet in Parliament. But there were many problems about the working of the constitution, and in particular, the extent of the Royal Prerogative that could only be worked out by trial and error. It could be said that we are still in the process of working them out today, with August 2013 simply the latest step on the road.

The Glorious Revolution had an immediate and dramatic effect on foreign policy. James II had been flirting with an alliance with Louis XIV (and indeed ended his life as an exile in his court). William III was a leader of the Protestant League and a committed enemy of France. Within days of his accession he had expelled the French ambassador and aligned England with the opponents of France. The country found itself locked in a major war with France. How had that come about?

William was on record as being a firm supporter of the Royal Prerogative. He remarked that, while monarchies and republics each had their good and bad points, no system of government was as bad as a monarchy without the necessary powers. The more extreme Whigs (William referred to them as 'republicans') favoured a severe limitation of the powers of the Crown. However, they were as strongly committed as the new King to the war with France; their very survival depended on defeating France, which stood for the restoration of James II, and with him the Jacobite Tories. So neither side could afford to push the dispute as to the extent of the Royal Prerogative too far.

The result was a typical British compromise. The Whigs allowed William to align England with the Dutch and to declare war on France without raising awkward questions about his power to do so unilaterally. William, recognising his dependence on Parliament for grants of finance to prosecute the war, gave ground on other important limitations of his prerogative: most notably Elizabeth I's jealously preserved power to prorogue or dismiss Parliament indefinitely, and Charles II's favoured device of leaving amenable parliaments sitting indefinitely. Thereafter, and to this day, Parliament has sat every year and, after a struggle, William finally gave his assent to an Act limiting the duration of any Parliament before fresh election to a maximum of three years (later seven, now a fixed period of five).

So, perhaps to an extent by accident, the Royal Prerogative to declare war survived the biggest constitutional upheaval since the Middle Ages entirely intact. That very much reflected the reality of the control of the military conduct of the war and of foreign policy, which William was determined to keep firmly in his own hands. He acted effectively as his own Prime Minister, took his own strategic decisions, conducted his own foreign policy and resisted repeated attempts by Parliament to exercise control over any of those areas. But at the same time his reign firmly and finally established the key instrument of parliamentary control – the annual appropriation of supply.

William was essentially a war leader as well as King. His successor, Queen Anne, James II's younger daughter, was not. She ruled to a much greater extent through her ministers (notably the Whig Godolphin and the Tory Harley), and during her reign, government by party started to take root. It is now that one can discern the emergence of the concept of a Cabinet, based in Parliament (though principally in the House of Lords) and exercising the powers of the Crown, though the Queen presided personally over Cabinet meetings and occasionally attended debates in the House of Lords. The boundaries were still being explored. On the one hand, her powers of expenditure were for the first time limited to the amount voted by parliamentary grant (known from then and until recently as 'the Civil List'). On the other, she was the last monarch (so far at least) to exercise her power of veto, when she refused in 1708 to sign into law a bill relating to the raising of Scottish militia. (She was also, incidentally, the last monarch to 'touch for the King's evil', a belief started in Edward the Confessor's reign that those suffering from scrofula would be cured by the touch of their sovereign – one of the very last such sufferers to be touched by Queen Anne, in 1712, being a 2-year-old Samuel Johnson.)

But as we shall see in the next section, the most significant fact about Queen Anne's reign – at least for our particular topic of the use of the Royal Prerogative to go to war – was her inability to produce a living heir.

The Act of Settlement 1701 – an Accidental Precedent for Parliamentary Restriction of the Royal Prerogative to Go to War

The Stuarts had not proved to be any better breeders than the Tudors. Mary II had died childless, and William III did not remarry. Despite seventeen pregnancies, Mary's younger sister, Queen Anne, had only one surviving child, her son William, who died of fever aged 11 in 1700. By then it was clear she was past childbearing. This created a crisis, since the Stuart in direct line of succession (assuming the rumour that he was a changeling smuggled into Queen Mary of Modena's bed in a warming pan was untrue) was James II's son, James Francis Edward Stuart, better known to history as 'The Old Pretender'; a Roman Catholic in exile in France and a focus for Jacobite rebellion. Urgent measures were required to safeguard the Protestant succession before Queen Anne died.

The Act of Settlement was duly passed in 1701, providing for the crown of England to pass to Sophia, Electress of Hanover, a granddaughter of James I and a firm Protestant, and her Protestant successors. In 1707, the Act of Union provided for the same succession to the throne of Scotland. This was another significant extension of the power of Parliament to dictate the succession to the throne. In the event, Sophia died two months before her cousin, Queen Anne, and the crown alighted upon the head of Sophia's son George I, a 54-year-old Protestant, foreign-born, German-speaking prince, already ruling the Electorate of Hanover in his own right. He was a great-grandson of James I and therefore had by blood a perfectly respectable claim to the throne, albeit inferior to the claims of some fifty Roman Catholic princes and princesses, including the Old Pretender and his son Charles, the Young Pretender – all barred from the succession by the prohibition of Catholics in the Act of Settlement.

As well as dictating who was and was not eligible for the throne of England (and shortly afterwards Scotland and later the self-governing Dominions), the Act of 1701 (parts of which remain in force to this day and form the bedrock of our modern constitutional structure) also formalised and reduced the powers of the Privy Council, and thereby accelerated the shift of power towards the Cabinet, which becomes significant in the later stages of our story.

However, for our immediate purposes, the Act of Settlement has a particular, though unrecognised, significance to the extent of the Royal Prerogative to declare war. The Act provides:

> That in case the Crown and imperial dignity of this Realm shall hereafter come to any person, not being a native of this Kingdom of England, this nation be not obliged to engage in any war for the defence of any dominions or territories which do not belong to the Crown of England, without the consent of Parliament.

The obvious intent of this provision was to prevent the Electors of Hanover employing British soldiers to fight their private dynastic wars on the Continent. However, its implications are much wider than that. Its effect is to prevent such a King from exercising his prerogative, whether through Council or Cabinet, to go to war in support of any ally facing attack, unless Parliament (not the Council or Cabinet) gives its consent. This represents a potentially huge diminution in the extent of the Royal Prerogative, though limited to the unusual circumstance of a foreign-born monarch.

The provision was, in the event, never put to the test. The last foreign-born King was George II and, due to the operation of the 'Salic Law', Victoria was barred from the succession in Hanover altogether. George II did, in fact, lead a mixed force of British and Hanoverian troops against the French during the War of the Austrian Succession, and in 1743 fought and won the Battle of Dettingen (becoming the last reigning King of England to date ever to personally command troops in battle), specifically in defence of Hanover. However, as the enemy was the French, nobody seems to have raised any constitutional objection.

The Act of Settlement continues to govern the succession to the thrones of the United Kingdom and all Commonwealth countries that still recognise the Queen as their head of state. Though never expressly acted upon, the provision referred to above appears to establish an important precedent for the reduction or oversight of the Royal Prerogative in future by Act of Parliament. A one-line amendment simply removing the words 'not being a native of this Kingdom of England' could provide a readymade law entirely subordinating the Royal Prerogative to go to war to the will of Parliament. Whether or not that is in fact a good idea is the subject of discussion in the earlier parts of this book. But it cannot be said that there is no precedent for Parliament interfering with the Royal Prerogative. By the odd accident of a ruling foreign Prince inheriting the crown of the United Kingdoms, we have a precedent of 307 years standing built into an existing Act of Parliament that constitutes one of the principal building blocks of the British Constitution – except that nobody so far seems to have noticed it.

War with the American Colonies – Dawn of the Modern Era

Great Britain stumbled into war with its American colonies between 1773, when the tax dispute in Boston got out of hand, and 1775 when the first shots were fired in earnest

Prime Minister Lord North (1732–1792), a dove forced from office for fighting a war too long.

at British garrison troops in Lexington. There was no question of anything as formal as a declaration of war. The colonists were in rebellion against the troops garrisoned in their colonies to enforce order, and the garrison commanders responded accordingly. As the rebellion and the fighting spread, more British troops were sucked in, initially those already in North America and then reinforcements sent from the home country.

Ironically the war was run by a War Cabinet under a Prime Minister, Lord North, who was reluctant to commit

to it. Despite that, the majority in Parliament and the country were strongly in favour of war and there was no question
raised about the deployment of troops and naval forces by
the Cabinet by exercise of the Royal Prerogative, and certainly no suggestion that Parliament had the right, or should
have the right, to a vote on whether or not such deployments
should be made in the first place. But the initial enthusiasm
for war steadily evaporated with Lord North's half-hearted
conduct of it. The mood of the country changed as the
campaign dragged on year after year, and parliamentary
opposition to North's administration grew. The political
situation came to a dramatic head after the defeat and surrender of Cornwallis at Yorktown in October 1781, and led
inexorably to North's resignation in March 1782.

It has been suggested by modern commentators, discussing the implications of what happened in the House of
Commons on 29 August 2013, that the events leading to
Lord North's political demise somehow provide a precedent
for parliamentary control of the Royal Prerogative to go
to war in the first place. However, if one properly dissects
the confused situation between October 1781 and March
1782, it is clear that they do no such thing. An important
precedent was indeed set in 1782, and was relied on repeatedly during the next two centuries as we shall see in the next
chapter, but not the one suggested. The precedent in fact
set was Parliament's power to remove a government that
is conducting a war which Parliament no longer supports.
To understand that distinction, and the implications of this
critically important milestone on the road towards parliamentary oversight of the war-making process, it is necessary
first to set out what actually happened in a little detail.

The order of events appears to have been as follows. In
November 1781, when North heard the disastrous news of
Cornwallis' surrender at Yorktown, he is reported to have
said: 'Oh God; it's all over',[15] and thereafter he sought to
resign. But George III would not countenance his resignation,
or any suggestion of peace with the colonies, or recognition

of their independence from the Crown. The war therefore continued in the face of mounting parliamentary opposition, and North had no choice but to soldier on at the will of his King, in the face of repeated hostile motions against his administration. Therefore, to all appearances, the Royal Prerogative to declare war (or peace) was still alive and well, and effectively provided the fetters that shackled the unfortunate North to the King's faltering war machine.

But the pressure in Parliament was relentless. In January 1782, a motion for a declaration that no more force should be used in America was moved in the House of Commons, but was defeated by 220 votes to 178. In February 1782, despite the recent naval victory against the French (key allies of the American rebels) in the West Indies, a motion for an immediate surrender was defeated by a majority of just one vote, but then a second similar motion a week later was passed by 234 votes to 215. North again tendered his resignation, but again it was not accepted by the King, who neither wanted to give up the colonies nor to appoint a new First Lord of the Treasury. So again, North had no choice but to continue in office, though his position was increasingly untenable.

On 15 March 1782 he survived a motion of censure, thanks to the support of a small group of independent MPs who, though opposed to the war, had no wish to see the Opposition in office. However, a week later it became clear that their support could not be relied upon and, faced with a further motion tabled against his administration, North finally forced the King to accept his resignation. He immediately announced it to a surprised House of Commons, who were digging in for an all-night debate, stepped into his carriage that he had waiting at the door of the House, and disappeared from history. The words of his resignation letter to the King are significant: 'Your Majesty is well apprised that in this country a prince on the throne cannot with prudence oppose the deliberate resolution of the House of Commons.'[16]

So, is this a precedent for the overruling by the will of Parliament of the Royal Prerogative to go to war? It is clearly no such thing. The war with the colonies was started by the forces of the Crown reacting to events on the ground without any intervention from Parliament, and was then carried on by the King's ministers in accordance with the King's will and in the face of mounting hostility in Parliament and the country. A clearer example of the working of the Prerogative in all its medieval glory could hardly be found. The shades of Edward I and Edward III would surely have been nodding approvingly, at least until March 1782.

But the events in Parliament in early 1782 do nevertheless represent a critical step forward in the development of parliamentary oversight of the war-making process, and one that held good for the next two centuries. The events leading up to Lord North's resignation, and the fall of his administration, demonstrate the first clear example of the working of the Constitution in the way it has always in modern times been understood to work, at least until 29 August 2013.

The King, through his appointed ministers in Parliament – the Cabinet – has the prerogative to go to war. Parliament has the power, developed in medieval times as we have seen, to vote or withhold supply, and therefore the effective power to control the continuance of the war itself. Parliament, through its ability to debate and pass motions, has the further power, developed during Stuart and Hanoverian times, to express its approval or disapproval of the war generally, and call ministers to account for their decisions. Parliament's final sanction, if it wholly disapproves of the war or the government's conduct of it, is to wield its ultimate weapons: the Motion of Censure and, finally, the Vote of No Confidence.

That was precisely the power wielded by Parliament for the first time against Lord North in the American War of Independence – though in the end, by forcing his own resignation and stepping smartly into his carriage before the House had a chance to vote, he managed to jump just before he was pushed. As it was the first time this weapon had been deployed, its effect was at first uncertain, due to the King's continuing personal involvement in the appointment and dismissal of his ministers. However, North was well aware of the impact of it, and said as much in his prescient letter to the King. He understood, as the King did not, that henceforth (if not before) neither the King nor his appointed ministers in Cabinet could hope to pursue a war, or indeed continue to govern at all, in opposition to the expressed will of Parliament. A new era had indeed dawned.

So 1782 is not a precedent for parliamentary control of the Royal Prerogative to go to war, as some have tried to present it. Rather it is an important precedent for the proposition, stated with admirable clarity by Alistair Burt (quoted on page 25), that it is for the government of the day to take the executive decision to take the country to war and it is for Parliament to approve or disapprove the government's actions by subsequent debate and votes, culminating if necessary with the final sanction of a Vote of No Confidence, thereby rendering it impossible for the government to continue in office.

That has been the generally accepted balance in modern times, at least into the present century, and that is the precedent that was set by Lord North's dramatic demise in 1782. It was, in truth, the dawn of the modern era, but it did not set any precedent for the issue under discussion in this book – the prerogative to take the country to war in the first place.

THE PREROGATIVE AND POPULAR DEMOCRACY

The Story So Far

The Royal Prerogative developed from its early emergence as a right of kings to command their subjects in war, limited initially only by the reach of royal power and then by the development of customary law and practice. As Parliament slowly emerged as a component in the governance of the country it gradually increased its power to rein in the unbridled appetite of kings for war, by increasing and formalising its hold over the funds needed for it.

With the reduction in the power of the landed feudal aristocracy during the blood-letting of the fifteenth century, we have seen power becoming increasingly centralised under the Crown, and decisions of war and peace firmly in the hands of the monarch and the Privy Council, with Parliament doggedly maintaining its right to criticise and advise, and its crucial power to control supply. The battle between kings, who saw their powers deriving from God not man, and parliaments, who were increasingly determined to establish independent privileges and powers not derived from the Crown, came to a violent head in the further bloodletting of the seventeenth century.

Thereafter, it was principally the accident of the lack of direct and acceptable heirs to the throne and the need to exclude Roman Catholics with foreign allegiances from the succession that gave Parliament an unprecedented

'The Crimean Scandal' – Evelyn Wood sketched the suffering of the ragged British soldier in the savage winter of 1854.

opportunity to move to centre stage. In return for accepting the rule of a chosen monarch, it took upon itself, for the first time in history, the power of selecting suitable candidates for the throne and offering them the crown, on conditions that limited their prerogatives by statute.

The last stage of the story so far, taking us to the end of the eighteenth century, has seen the steady development of the independent power of Parliament and the emergence of ministers, appointed by the Crown but sitting in Parliament, exercising the powers formerly exercised by the Privy Council but relying for their continued ability to govern on commanding a majority in Parliament, and increasingly in the House of Commons.

By the end of the eighteenth century the procedure for declaring and conducting wars was, at least in retrospect, emerging pretty clearly, and continued to hold good for the next 200 or so years during the development of parliamentary democracy in the form we know it today. The constitutional power to take the country to war remains unchanged: war is declared pursuant to the Royal Prerogative as it always had been, though now exercised in the monarch's name by the Prime Minister with the support of Cabinet rather than by the monarch directly with the support of Council.

The constitutional reality, however, is, as Lord North recognised and explained to George III in his letter of resignation, that no government can take the country to war, and hope to sustain that war, without the broad support of the House of Commons. If the government of the day were to embark on a war of which the majority of the House of Commons disapproved, its sanction is clear and immediate: a Vote of No Confidence in the government would lead to the immediate fall of that government and the appointment of a new one that commanded the confidence of the House. That government would then be free to exercise the prerogative of bringing the war to an end. That is the clear pattern that we see operating through the ensuing 231 years from 1782, though coming under increasing challenge from thoughtful constitutional commentators and politicians by the end of the twentieth century.

1793 – Response to the Threat from Revolutionary France

The next step in our review of the Royal Prerogative is provided, just for a change, by the French. When revolution broke out in France in 1789, opinion in Britain and elsewhere was sharply divided. Some parliamentarians like Edmund Burke were concerned about the potential for constitutional anarchy: 'I cannot conceive how any man can have brought himself to that pitch of presumption, to consider his country as nothing but "carte blanche", upon which he may scribble whatever he pleases.'[1] Others agreed with William Wordsworth that 'Bliss was it in that dawn to be alive, but to be young was very heaven!'[2] Even Leopold of Austria, the younger brother of Marie Antoinette, who succeeded his elder brother to the throne of Austria and the Holy Roman Empire in 1790, at first looked on the Revolution with equanimity, believing it to be in the hands of responsible constitutional reformers. However, as it entered its more radical and violent phases, along with the rest of the crowned heads of Europe he quickly changed his view, and even before the revolutionaries chopped off the heads of his sister and brother-in-law, war was seen as inevitable.

To save Leopold the trouble, Revolutionary France declared war on Austria first, shortly followed by Prussia. After the regicide, Spain and Portugal joined the anti-French coalition, and on 1 February 1793 France declared war on Great Britain and the Dutch Republic. There was, therefore, no call for the exercise of the Royal Prerogative on this occasion – Great Britain was at war whether she liked it or not.

It was, however, the occasion for an immediate debate in Parliament to decide whether or not the House of Commons was prepared to support the government in its prosecution of the war. In debate in the House after the start of the war in 1793, William Pitt argued in favour of pursuing the war as the only way to ensure a 'secure and lasting peace'. He was opposed by Charles James Fox, who continued to support the French Revolution long after more moderate opinion was repelled by its violence and arbitrary executions. Fox argued that the war was ideological, aimed at restoring the French monarchy and could not justify the miseries and restrictions to liberty the war would inevitably impose on British people. Edmund Burke, who had by this time crossed the floor to support Pitt, responded that it was precisely because it was ideological that he supported the war. The government carried the House with a very large majority and continued to command overwhelming support despite the necessity of introducing oppressive measures including the Combination Acts and even the suspension of habeas corpus in 1794 to suppress sedition, coupled with sharply increasing taxation to pay for the war.

A large majority of the political nation recognised that Pitt was the only man with the force and authority to lead the country in resisting French aggression, while the radical elements became ever more extreme, with Fox going as far as expressing pleasure in seeing France gain advantage over England as long as English policy remained so mistaken. In the face of imminently expected invasion prior to Nelson's great victory at Trafalgar in 1805, this seemed to most people dangerously close to treason and the majority preferred to stick with Pitt and the defence of the realm.

But the real point of importance is that it was, by now, clear beyond argument that the ability to continue with the war depended wholly on securing and maintaining the support of the majority of the House of Commons. Had Pitt lost the debate in 1793, or any major motion thereafter, there can be no doubt that he could not have continued to prosecute the war, and he would have had no choice but to resign. The pattern set in 1782 was unchallengeable, but was in the event not put to the test.

1853 – The Crimea: The Prerogative Preserved but Parliament Shows its Teeth (Again)

In 1853 Russia went to war with the Ottoman Empire, ostensibly over the rights of Russian Orthodox worshippers in the Turkish-controlled Holy Land. Russia quickly destroyed the Ottoman fleet in the Black Sea and looked set to bring down the tottering Ottoman Empire, pick up the remains, and establish itself as a force in the Eastern Mediterranean. For a combination of motives, both expressed and unexpressed and which are far outside the confines of this book, France and then Britain became steadily more involved until they declared war on Russia on 27 and 28 March 1854 respectively.

The Prime Minister, Lord Aberdeen, at the head of a coalition government which included Lord Palmerston, Lord John Russell and Gladstone, made the formal declaration of war by means of the Royal Prerogative in the traditional way. A formal ultimatum from the governments of the Emperor of France and the Queen of Great Britain was delivered to the Czar by an officer of the Royal Navy called Captain Blackwood. The Czar declined to answer it and a state of war with Russia therefore existed. This was reported to Parliament by means of a Royal Message from Queen Victoria, read to the House of Lords by Lord Aberdeen and to the House of Commons by Lord John Russell on Tuesday 28 March, followed by a public announcement in the *London Gazette*. A similar message from Emperor Louis Napoleon was read to the French Senate. The Queen's message set out the proposed 'active steps to oppose the encroachments of Russia upon Turkey' and Friday 31 March was fixed as the date for Parliament to debate the issue and reply to the message.

During the debate, opposition to the war in principle, rather than to the proposed means of prosecuting it, was expressed by certain groups in the House of Commons, principally the Cobdenites, but a large majority of both Houses expressed support for the government. Within a few months however, after the battles of Alma, Balaclava and Inkerman, the bogging down of the army in front of Sevastopol and the appalling failures of organisation and supply during the winter of 1854, extreme dissatisfaction was being expressed in all quarters at the way the war was being conducted.

Matters came to a head in Parliament after reports began to be gathered revealing the extent of mismanagement in the Crimea and fingers were pointed increasingly at the government. On 28 January 1855 John Arthur Roebuck introduced a motion for the appointment of a Select Committee to enquire into the conduct of the war. This motion was carried by the large majority of 305 in favour and 148 against. Lord Aberdeen, struggling to hold the competing personalities within his coalition cabinet together, treated this as a Vote of No Confidence in his government and very correctly resigned. The Queen, desperate to avoid sending for Lord Palmerston, invited first Lord Derby and then Lord Lansdowne to form administrations. Both offered positions to Palmerston which he agreed conditionally to accept, but both failed to muster the necessary support, and eventually the Queen was left with nowhere else to turn. Palmerston, immensely popular in the country, became Prime Minister at the age of 71 and quickly rallied support in Parliament for continuation of the war.

So the Crimean War provides a textbook example of the unwritten but robust balance between the Royal Prerogative to take the country to war on the one hand, and parliamentary control over its continuation and conduct and ultimately over the survival of the government conducting the war on the other, that was established by 1782 and survived more or less intact until 29 August 2013.

1914 – The Royal Prerogative Undimmed

The declaration of war against Germany on 4 August 1914 would not have raised an eyebrow in any medieval or Tudor court. The Royal Prerogative was operated exactly as it had been by Edward III or Henry VIII or Elizabeth I, and applied throughout the British Empire. It is true that before war was formally declared the question was placed before the House of Commons on 3 August 1914 just to ensure that the government had its support, but that was not seen by anybody as giving Parliament the power to decide whether the country should go to war or not. A short summary of events leading up to the declaration will help put the matter into context.

By the Treaty of London in 1839 the European powers, including Great Britain, France, Germany and Austria, had guaranteed the neutrality of the new kingdom of Belgium. Following the assassination of Archduke Franz Ferdinand at Sarajevo on 28 June and the resulting stand-off between

Hold every front page in the world.

Austria, Serbia and Russia, the Germans became involved on Austria's side and the French on Russia's and finally, on 3 August 1914, Germany declared war on France. A few hours later France declared war on Germany. In response, Germany initiated the Schlieffen Plan, which involved its northern army corps swinging through Belgium, thereby violating Belgium's neutrality. On the same day, by a majority, the British Cabinet resolved to honour its treaty obligations to Belgium and made certain ill-defined promises of support to the French. That was the extent of the full Cabinet's direct involvement in the decision. However, before the fatal decision was finally taken to go to war, the matter was put before the House of Commons by the Foreign Secretary, Sir Edward Grey.

The House had been recalled, unusually, in August, and sat even more unusually in the early afternoon of Bank Holiday Monday, 3 August to hear the Foreign Secretary make a detailed statement to the House. It is worth quoting some extracts from it:

> Last week I stated that we were working for peace not only for this country, but to preserve the peace of Europe. Today events move so rapidly that it is exceedingly difficult to state with technical accuracy the actual state of affairs, but it is clear that the peace of Europe cannot be preserved ... Before I proceed to state the position of His Majesty's Government I would like to clear the ground so that, before I come to state to the House what our attitude is with regard to the present crisis, the House may know exactly under what obligations the government is, or the House can be said to be, in coming to a decision on the matter.[3]

He then read out several of the diplomatic notes that had passed between the government and the British ambassadors in the European capitals and said:

I read that to the House, not as a declaration of war on our part, not as entailing immediate aggressive action on our part, but as binding us to take aggressive action should that contingency arise. Things move very hurriedly from hour to hour.

In other words, he was giving a summary of the fast-moving diplomatic situation in order to inform the House as far as possible what had happened to enable them to debate the matter thereafter. He went on:

What other policy is there before the House? ... We have made the commitment to France that I have read to the House ...

The most awful responsibility is resting upon the Government in deciding what to advise the House of Commons to do. We have disclosed our minds to the House of Commons. We have disclosed the issue, the information which we have, and made clear to the House, I trust, that we are prepared to face that situation ...

We are now face to face with a situation and all the consequences which it may yet have to unfold. We believe we shall have the support of the House at large in proceeding to whatever the consequences may be and whatever measures may be forced upon us by the development of facts or action taken by others. I believe the country, so quickly has the situation been forced upon it, has not had time to realise the issue.

It was then agreed that the House would rise and reconvene that evening for a debate upon the question: 'That this House do now adjourn.' In other words, an adjournment debate – the usual mechanism to give the House the opportunity to debate an issue without any specific motion for any specific steps to be taken.

There followed a two-hour debate, preceded by a short update from the Foreign Secretary explaining events since his statement in the afternoon. The debate itself is notable for a number of things. First, neither the Prime Minister, nor the Foreign Secretary after he had made his short statement, nor any member of the Cabinet, appear even to have been present in the House. Second, almost every member who spoke, mostly from the Labour benches, spoke in opposition to the war in principle or to the adequacy of the steps taken by the government to avoid it. Third, no one from the government benches (or indeed the Leader of His Majesty's Opposition, Mr Bonar Law) spoke in reply or summed up at the end. Fourth, the debate was brought to an end by Arthur Balfour, a senior Tory statesman, who supported the government but who himself appears only to have been in the chamber towards the end. It is worth recording at some length extracts of what he said, as he summed up exactly the limitations of the parliamentary device of an adjournment debate, and expressed the generally held view of the extent and limitations of the role of Parliament in the lead up to war:

We are not discussing in any effective sense the policy of His Majesty's government. We are not dealing with any resolution that touches the policy of His Majesty's government. The question before the House is not the policy of His Majesty's government, but the adjournment of the House; an adjournment that must take place in the ordinary course, seeing that all the business of the House is now concluded.

... On that question I do not think even in ordinary circumstances that it would be possible to have an effective discussion or come to any resolution ... We know perfectly well this is not a debate upon the tremendous national issue brought before us earlier in the day ...

All I say is that this is not a debate on the great question before the country. It does not represent what the House of Commons thinks on the question, and I say, under these circumstances, lest some general misconception ... should obtain currency at home and abroad, I would venture very respectfully to suggest, in the general interest, that this debate should be brought to a close.

Let the house remember that the Prime Minister at half-past four o clock promised a full opportunity for debating the policy of the Government. That will come. I do not know exactly what the occasion chosen by the Prime Minister will be, but I imagine it would ... come upon some Vote of Credit asked from this House for dealing with a great national emergency. Then is the opportunity for the House, by speech, and by vote, worthy of the great occasion on which it will have to pronounce, to say what it has to say and vote as it desires to vote ...[4]

Balfour, a trusted and experienced statesman and former Prime Minister, and later a successful Foreign Secretary, knew exactly what he was talking about. The passages set out above encapsulate the constitutional position as it had developed since the Middle Ages, and as it had been understood since at least 1782, and as it continued to be understood at least until 2003 and generally until 29 August 2013. The government of the day was responsible for the executive steps leading up to war, with Parliament having the expectation and right of being kept informed as far as possible as events unfolded, and being given the opportunity to express its views. The declaration itself was, as it always had been, a matter for the Royal Prerogative, exercised in the name of the King on the decision of the appointed ministers of the Crown. Parliament would then immediately have the right to debate the issue of the war, to vote on supply and at any time to exercise its final sanction of dismissing the government through the mechanism of the Vote of No Confidence, as it had done to Lord North in 1782 and to Lord Aberdeen in 1855.

Events after 3 August 1914 unfolded rapidly and in exact accordance with that understanding. The Foreign Secretary, Grey, in consultation with the Prime Minister, Asquith, but no one else, sent an ultimatum to Germany requiring it by 11.00 p.m. Greenwich Mean Time (midnight in Germany) on 4 August to halt its invasion of Belgium. At 10.30 p.m. King George V convened a meeting of the Privy Council at Buckingham Palace. No member of the Cabinet, not even the Prime Minister or the Foreign Secretary, were present. The Privy Council duly authorised a proclamation of a state of war with Germany effective from 11.00 p.m. that night, and the King signed it.

By that single proclamation, made by the King exercising the same prerogative through the same Council by which Elizabeth had declared war with Spain 325 years earlier, the United Kingdom of Great Britain and Ireland, the Dominions of Canada, Australia, New Zealand and South Africa, the British Imperial possessions in India and the British colonial possessions in Africa, the Caribbean and elsewhere throughout the Empire all instantly found themselves in a state of war with Germany.

The Parliament of the United Kingdom had no say in the declaration, though two days later on 6 August, as envisaged by Balfour in his speech, the House of Commons had the opportunity to debate and approve (in Balfour's words) a 'Vote of Credit' –i.e. supply. The House signified its approval of the war by voting, without division, an immediate credit of £100 million to finance its prosecution. Neither the governments nor the parliaments of the Dominions were consulted or informed in advance. The Canadian Parliament alone subsequently passed a motion expressing its approval. The Governors General (the King's Representatives) in each Dominion simply echoed the Royal Proclamation, as did the Viceroy of India. The colonies simply did what they were told. (Ironically, probably the first shot in the naval war between Britain and Germany was fired by the only British gunboat on Lake Nyasa, whose commander, Captain Rhoades, received news of the outbreak of war by telegram just before his German counterpart, Captain Berndt, the commander of the only German gunboat on the lake. Rhoades rowed over to the

German ship, invited its Captain over for tea, informed him that a state of war existed between them, and then opened fire and sank the German's vessel in front of his eyes.)

Thus, by powers developed by medieval monarchs were upwards of 400 million people summarily committed to a cataclysmic war against a country of which the majority of them had almost certainly never heard.

1939 – No Change at Home

The lead up to war against Germany on 3 September 1939 was rather more protracted than in 1914, but the powers employed to declare war in the United Kingdom were essentially the same. Parliament met on 24 August and passed an Emergency Powers Act. On 25 August an Anglo-Polish treaty of mutual assistance was signed (complete with a clause guaranteeing the Danzig Corridor, kept secret from Hitler to avoid annoying him). As a result Hitler postponed his invasion of Poland, and Halifax, the Foreign Secretary, urged the Polish government to negotiate. They refused and German troops finally crossed the Polish frontier on 1 September. The Poles immediately appealed to their new ally, but Halifax was keen to delay any ultimatum in the hope of setting up an international conference to discuss the issue without time constraints. The Cabinet, however, insisted that German troops must be withdrawn first as a condition of any such conference.

Eventually the Prime Minister, Neville Chamberlain, went before the House of Commons to explain the prospects of a conference with the condition that Hitler must 'agree' to withdraw his troops – rather than actually do so. This was not well received by the House. Arthur Greenwood, acting Labour leader, rose to speak, to the famous (though unrecorded) exhortation from Leo Amery on the Tory benches to 'Speak for England, Arthur!'[5] The House broke up without any division, Greenwood told

Chamberlain that, without a declaration, 'it would be impossible to hold the House' and a deputation of ministers urged Chamberlain to declare war at once. The Cabinet met at 11.00 p.m., Halifax persuaded the Prime Minister to delay until next morning, and the ultimatum was delivered on 3 September at 9.00 a.m., expiring at 11.00 a.m. The Prime Minister formally announced the declaration of war by radio at 11.15 a.m. in the well-known words:

> I am speaking to you from the cabinet room at 10 Downing Street. This morning the British Ambassador in Berlin handed the German Government a final note stating that, unless we heard from them by 11 o'clock that they were prepared at once to withdraw their troops from Poland, a state of war would exist between us. I have to tell you now that no such undertaking has been received, and that consequently this country is at war with Germany.[6]

Closely following the pattern set in August 1914, on the afternoon of 3 September 1939, after the declaration of war, the Prime Minister made what Hansard describes as an 'Announcement to Parliament.' He spoke briefly, told the House that they were 'not in possession of all the information which we have', and advised that a state of war with Germany was in existence. The Opposition, in voicing their support, nonetheless warned that they would be scrutinising the government's actions with care. Mr Arthur Greenwood said:

> The Prime Minister has given us his word that Nazism will be overthrown, and as long as that relentless purpose is pursued with vigour, with foresight and with determination by the Government, so long will there be a united nation. But should there be confused councils, inefficiency and wavering, then other men must be called to take their places.[7]

There was no vote on the 'Announcement', the Prime Minister rather wearily winding up the debate by saying 'May I appeal to the House to bring these proceedings to a close? There is an immense amount of work to be done, and I am extremely anxious to get it through.' A number of orders pursuant to the war followed, but the House did not divide on any of them.

In other words, despite much greater involvement by Parliament in the lead-up to the declaration, the formal declaration of war in Britain when it finally came was made as a purely executive act by the Cabinet by means of the Royal Prerogative, just as it had been in 1914 and before.

1939 – All Change in the Dominions: Several Precedents for Parliamentary Control of the Prerogative

The position in the Dominions in 1939 differed significantly from that in 1914. Then, as we have seen, a single declaration by the King in Council had sufficed to commit the whole of the British Empire to war. But since the implementation of the Statute of Westminster in 1931, the Dominions had had internal self-government under the Crown, so that Britain's declaration of war in September 1939 no longer automatically bound them. Constitutionally they were free to make their own decisions. Their different responses to the crisis set some potentially significant precedents for the future of the Royal Prerogative. It is worth looking at each of them separately.

The government of Australia followed Britain immediately without consulting its Parliament. Robert Menzies, Prime Minister of Australia, simply announced to the Australian people:

> Fellow Australians, it is my melancholy duty to inform you officially, that in consequence of a persistence by Germany

A British Indian Army soldier arrives at Singapore – and according to the
original caption, 'his "V" is backed by a million Indian troops and the rest of
the Empire as well.'

in her invasion of Poland, Great Britain has declared war
upon her and that, as a result, Australia is also at war.[8]

The words 'as a result' are obviously significant. His view
therefore appears to have been that nothing had changed
constitutionally at all since 1914, and that a declaration by
the King was a declaration binding upon all his subjects.

The government of New Zealand took the same view,
and coordinated its declaration to coincide with that of
Great Britain. Due to static over the short-wave radio and
a muddle over time zones, there is a long-standing theory
that New Zealand actually declared war before Britain.
However, the intention clearly was to do so jointly.

The government of Canada, though not constitutionally obliged to do so, decided to seek approval from both
houses of Parliament before declaring war. Parliament
was recalled on an emergency basis on 7 September and
the issue was debated in both houses. The Senate gave its
approval to a declaration of war on 8 September, and the
House of Commons a day later. Only then did the Prime
Minister, Mackenzie King, and the Cabinet draft an Order
in Council to that effect. Canadian diplomats then took the
document to King George VI at Windsor for his signature
on 10 September, and only then was Canada officially at
war with Germany. The Canadian government's official
recorder noted: 'King George VI of England did not ask
us to declare war for him – we asked King George VI of
Canada to declare war for us.'[9]

The government of South Africa had a much more con-
voluted route to war. The Prime Minister, Hertzog, a Boer
with long-standing anti-British and pro-German sympa-
thies, wished the country to remain neutral. The issue was
put before Parliament, and Parliament resolved to go to
war by 80 votes to 67. Hertzog then went to the Governor
General (the King's representative in South Africa) and
asked for a dissolution. The Governor General refused and
invited the pro-British Smuts, a long-standing friend of

Winston Churchill, to form a government. He duly became Prime Minister and war was declared against Germany on 6 September.

The government of Eire went a step further. The Anglo-Irish treaty of 1921 declared Ireland to be a 'sovereign, independent and democratic state', but its status was still that of a Dominion with internal self-government under the Crown. Its hard-line, anti-British, republican-minded Prime Minister, Eamonn de Valera, took full advantage of the Statute of Westminster. The Dáil was convened on 1 September 1939, and an Emergency Powers Act was passed to enforce whatever measures might become necessary. The country then declared itself neutral and used the powers to enforce rigid neutrality throughout the war.

All those events, but perhaps the Canadian experience in particular, represent a precedent of obvious significance for the present debate over the extent and exercise of the Royal Prerogative. In Canada the Prime Minister and Cabinet, exercising the executive powers of the Crown, chose to grant Parliament the right to debate and vote on the issue of going to war, before it was declared. Once approval of both houses was obtained, the government invited the King, as King of Canada, to make the declaration of war by Order in Council on its behalf. So the prerogative was still recognised but, in an act of self-denial, submitted by the Executive for prior approval by Parliament. That, essentially, may have been what the Cameron government were trying, in a muddled way, to grope their way towards on 29 August 2013. If so, they might have benefited from a short study of imperial history. We still have a long way to go.

1939 to 1945 – Parliamentary Oversight of the Conduct of War

The right of Parliament to control supply had, as we have seen, developed steadily since the emergence of Parliament itself in the Middle Ages. The right of Parliament to oversee the government's conduct of the war, and if necessary remove the government altogether if it felt that it was not up to the job, developed more slowly, but was demonstrated in 1782 and firmly established by 1855. Those rights continued to be juggled and balanced at important stages during the Second World War. A few brief examples will suffice.

During the Adjournment debate (on which, as explained above, a substantive vote is not possible) after the invasion of Norway on 9 April 1940, the Prime Minister was clear about the extent of the Royal Prerogative:

> His Majesty's Government have decided forthwith to extend their full aid to Norway ... Powerful units of the Navy are at sea. Hon. Members will realise that it would not be in the public interest to give details at this stage.[10]

'The Big Three' decide the fate of the world at the Yalta Conference. One of the three was not quite as 'big' as the other two.

There was some quibbling about it, and even the suggestion (which was not carried out) that a vote against the motion 'That This House do now adjourn' would send a particular message of disquiet about the Prime Minister's views. But again, the prime ministerial use of the Royal Prerogative to dispatch the forces prevailed.

There were, of course, a great many debates – and further statements – on a whole variety of military topics during the course of the war. There was a two-day debate and a vote, for example, on 6 May 1941, on 'sending assistance to Greece, and expressing confidence that operations in the Middle East and other theatres of war would be pursued with the utmost vigour'. But throughout the war, despite many irritable and argumentative debates, there was never any which would have resulted in anything other than overwhelming, wholehearted support for everything which the Prime Minister, the government and the armed forces were doing. In a very real sense, Parliament and the people were unanimous. And that unanimity allowed the extensive use of prime ministerial statements to keep the House 'informed' (rather than 'consulted about') military developments. The constitutional boundaries were never seriously put to the test.

MODERN TIMES: THE PREROGATIVE CHALLENGED

In the post-war era we find Parliament firmly in control, with the House of Commons ascendant and, after the emergencies of the 1930s and '40s, two-party politics back as the norm (at least until May 2010). The country is governed by the leader of the party with a clear majority in the House of Commons, by convention invariably appointed by the Queen to be Prime Minister, and his or her Cabinet chosen from the leading ranks of the party. The ancient prerogative powers of the Crown still underpin a large part of the executive powers of government, even though those powers are now exercised almost entirely by the elected government through Cabinet.

In most day-to-day circumstances the system works well and without controversy. Despite that, the last half-century has seen a dramatic increase in the number of legal challenges to the exercise of executive prerogative powers by means of the newly invigorated machinery of judicial review – all in all a healthy sign of a developing democracy. With such challenges to the exercise of executive prerogative power generally increasing, it was inevitable that the particular executive power under discussion, the exercise of the Royal Prerogative to take the country to war, would also come under increasing challenge.

This chapter will chart the progress of those challenges from the end of the Second World War until the start of the Iraq War in 2003. Various developments and events in that period may be seen as dress rehearsals for the moment on 29 August 2013 when 1,000 years of laborious constitutional development were casually consigned to the dustbin with the Prime Minister's unconsidered but unconditional surrender of the Royal Prerogative to the members of the House of Commons – who between them, predictably enough, succeeded only in dropping the ball.

1950 – The Korean War: A Chance to Vote, Though After the Event

In June 1950 North Korea invaded South Korea, and a United Nations Resolution was quickly passed (thanks to Stalin's helpful decision to boycott the organisation, thereby rendering it impossible to exercise the USSR's veto) calling on all member states to 'furnish assistance to the Republic of Korea as may be necessary to repel the armed attack and to restore international peace and security in the area'. The British Commonwealth responded by deploying British, Canadian, Australian and New Zealand forces already in the area in support of the US-dominated UN forces. This was the first time that Britain had gone to war in response to a United Nations Resolution – the requirement for which, as a pre-condition for going to war, was to become a topic for hot debate on future occasions. There was no formal declaration of war against North Korea, the authority for the deployment of troops deriving solely from the authority of the UN Resolution.

The Prime Minister, Clement Attlee, allowed a full-scale parliamentary debate on 5 July 1950 on the crisis. The debate was on the motion:

> That this House fully supports the action taken by His Majesty's Government in conformity with their obligations under the United Nations Charter, in helping to resist the unprovoked aggression against the Republic of Korea.[1]

A pacifist amendment was tabled, although not in the event voted on, and the government motion was carried without a division.

It is noteworthy that the debate took place on such a motion, giving the House of Commons the opportunity to vote against it, if it so chose, rather than simply on the usual motion to adjourn. Nevertheless, the critical point is that the motion was only proposed and debated after the action had started. It was designed simply to endorse prime ministerial action in sending the troops to war. As Mr Attlee said: 'I am asking the House to support the government in the action which they have taken.'[2] One has to assume that, in the unlikely event the House had divided and then voted down the motion, Mr Attlee, like Lords North and Aberdeen before him, would have had no option but to treat it as a confidence issue and resign.

The Leader of the Opposition, Winston Churchill, perhaps feeling left out of the loop after being accustomed for so long to be controlling events, asked that the House should meet in secret, so that the Prime Minister could share his intelligence on the matter – a request politely declined. That is a proposal which Mr Blair should perhaps have considered rather than trying to 'spin' the intelligence to justify the Iraq War in 2003. Churchill nonetheless accepted the risks to morale and to the conduct of the war if the House were not to endorse the Prime Minister's decision. His speech has echoes of that of his former friend and colleague, Arthur Balfour, in the adjournment debate on 3 August 1914. Churchill said:

> We consider that the Government were right to place a motion asking for approval in general terms ... There are grave dangers as we learned in the War [he was presumably referring to the Second World War], that false impressions may be created abroad by a debate prominently occupied by a handful of dissentients. It is better to have a division so that everyone can know how the

House of Commons stands and in what proportion. Should such a division occur, we on this side will vote with the Government. [However he did add:] I cannot overlook the fact that in giving our support we run some party and political risks.[3]

But the House did not, in the end, divide. In other words, while it is significant that, unlike the First and Second World Wars, there was a substantive debate with at least the theoretical possibility of a vote, the reality was that with the nation already at war, anything other than overwhelming support for the Prime Minister, and for our forces in action, would have been politically impossible. As we shall see, this procedure was further developed during the Falklands crisis thirty-two years later.

1956 – The Suez Crisis: Business as Usual

Sir Anthony Eden's government reverted to tradition before the disastrous Anglo-French intervention in Suez, after Colonel Nasser's nationalisation of the canal. Following well-established precedent, there was only an adjournment debate on the crisis on 2 August 1956, during which the Prime Minister said that:

In view of the uncertain situation created by the actions of the Egyptian Government, Her Majesty's Government have thought it necessary – and I wanted to take this first opportunity to tell the House – to take certain precautionary measures of a military nature.[4]

There was, of course, no vote possible. Thereafter it took a 'Private Notice Question' (a then rarely granted opportunity for a backbencher or HM Opposition to call the government to account)[5] to force the government to come back to the House on 26 November 1956 to answer the question:

What action the Secretary of State for Foreign Affairs proposes to take as a result of the Egyptian decision to expel all British and French nationals from Egypt, and how many people are affected?

The Minister of State for Foreign Affairs tried, rather inadequately, to answer it on behalf of the government, and only a very short debate was allowed.

Apart from that rather unusual and pretty insignificant innovation, the brief intervention in Suez did not mark any development in the balance between Crown and Parliament before the Americans precipitately (some would say short-sightedly) waved their economic truncheon and forced the British government into a humiliating climb-down.

1982 – The Falklands Invaded: the Empire, and the Prerogative, Strike Back

After various early-warning signals were missed, resulting in the very honourable resignation of the Foreign Secretary Lord Carrington, the Argentine Junta invaded the British Falkland Islands on 2 April 1982. On 3 April the United Nations Security Council by a majority (with four abstentions and Panama the only vote against) passed Resolution 502 demanding the immediate withdrawal of all Argentine forces and calling on both governments to seek a diplomatic solution and refrain from further military action.

The British Prime Minister, Margaret Thatcher, relying on the first part of Resolution 502 and determinedly ignoring the second, simply informed Parliament on 3 April 1982 that all necessary steps would be taken to restore the sovereignty of the Falkland Islands and their dependent territories. Then on 5 April, having taken advice from the military High Command, she announced to the nation the dispatch of the Task Force. There was no formal declaration of war by Great Britain against Argentina and the operation

Falklands, 1982 – an unequivocal use of the Royal Prerogative.

was restricted to re-establishing Britain's sovereignty over its territories in the Falkland Islands, South Georgia and the Sandwich Islands, which it achieved in less than ten weeks. However, it is clear that the ordering of British forces into action in the South Atlantic was carried out, and can only have been carried out, by means of the Royal Prerogative.

The mechanism employed on 3 April for informing Parliament of the government's intentions was once again an adjournment debate, the House having been recalled – most unusually – on a Saturday. There were subsequently a total of fourteen statements and a further five adjournment debates on the subject before the Argentinian surrender in June, but none of them took the form of substantive motions that could have resulted in a hostile vote.

Unlike Korea, when the Prime Minister had put forward a substantive motion inviting support that would, at least in theory, have allowed the House to vote against it, no such opportunity was offered by Margaret Thatcher this time. That may well be explained by the fact that the Opposition were considerably less robust in their support for the Prime Minister than they had been in previous wars. There were those reliable voices of dissent such as Tony Benn and Tam Dalyell, (who between them have spoken up against nearly every military involvement of the last sixty years or so). There were calls for example from Denis Healey for Mrs Thatcher's resignation following that of Lord Carrington:

> The Right Hon. Lady has chosen to stay, but from this moment she has no moral or political right whatsoever to ask the Opposition to give her a blank cheque ... No responsible Opposition in this situation could surrender their freedom of thought and action to a Prime Minister who had demonstrated such a monumental lack of judgement.[6]

Mr Healey, nonetheless, ended up giving the government his grudging support – thereby producing a serious anticlimax to his somewhat intemperate attack:

> This has put the Opposition in the unenviable position of supporting the nation's interest, even when that interest is represented abroad by a Cabinet that has lost its authority at home. Nevertheless we shall support that Government's efforts to resolve the crisis.

It was clear, however, that the majority of the House were broadly in support, and the tenor of most speeches reflected that. As the young Winston Churchill put it, with memorable overtones of his grandfather fifty years previously:

> Let there be no flinching or faltering in our resolve as the moment for decisive action draws near. There must be no doubt in Buenos Aires or in Washington about

the determination of the British Parliament and nation to free our people from fascist rule. Let the word go out from this House today that the nation stands united behind the Government, and above all behind the forces of the Crown in that resolve. We wish all those who sail with the fleet Godspeed, a victorious outcome and a safe return.[7]

A senior Conservative backbencher, John Stokes, who had seen service and been wounded during the Second World War, succinctly summarised the modern understanding of the continuing tension between Royal Prerogative and parliamentary oversight:

It is of course right that we have been recalled, and that we should be kept informed by Her Majesty's Government about what is happening. Parliaments in the past were an awful nuisance to kings when they were conducting difficult diplomatic negotiations. Queen Elizabeth I took a very severe view when Parliament interfered in foreign affairs. I am sure that many modern Governments must have felt the same.[8]

So in the 1980s the constitutional procedure, developed over centuries and firmly established by the end of the eighteenth century, still held good. The government took the decision to respond militarily to the crisis in question and the Prime Minister successfully sought the support of the House for whatever decisions it chose to take. The adjournment debate on 3 April took place before the Task Force actually sailed but there was no suggestion that the House was being called upon to decide whether or not it should be dispatched. Once it was steaming towards the South Atlantic, anything other than support was (as Denis Healey recognised) politically impossible. Parliament in the era of mass communication appeared increasingly as little more than a backdrop for statements to the media and nation.

1991 – The First Gulf War: Korea Revisited, with a Twist

On 2 August 1990 Iraq invaded Kuwait. The response of the international community was immediate, with a series of United Nations resolutions, starting with Resolution 660, demanding immediate withdrawal of all Iraqi troops, and followed by others imposing steadily escalating sanctions. They culminated in UN Resolution 678, which gave Iraq until 15 January 1991 to withdraw from Kuwait, and authorised member states to use 'all necessary means to uphold and implement Resolution 660' – i.e. carte blanche authority to use military force to eject Iraqi troops after that deadline expired.

Meanwhile a vast coalition of forces had been accumulated in Saudi Arabia and around Iraq, dominated by the United States, who contributed 73 per cent of the total forces, but with significant contributions from the United Kingdom, with over 10 per cent of the total, alongside thirty-three other countries. The air campaign commenced on 17 January 1991, allied land forces crossed the Kuwaiti border on 24 February, Kuwait was liberated on 27 February and the ceasefire was announced by President Bush about 100 hours later.

The precedent set by Korea in 1950 was closely followed, though with an interesting twist at the end that perhaps presaged the constitutional storm gathering in, and after, 2003. Like Korea, the authority to go to war was founded on the UN Resolution, and there was again no formal declaration of war. British troops joined the UN coalition and went into action with the rest. There were several parliamentary debates during the course of the developing crisis in the second half of 1990. Then, on 15 January 1991, the day the UN deadline expired and when war was now inevitable, the House of Commons held the – by now customary – adjournment debate, starting with a detailed statement from the Prime Minister (by now John Major, in place of Margaret Thatcher who had played a critical international role in the early stages of the crisis) and continuing with speeches from all sides of the House, including those opposed in principle to the war or to the involvement in it of the USA. Then, on 17 January 1991, when the air war actually started, the Prime Minister made a short statement informing the House of the commencement of hostilities a few hours earlier, reporting the loss of one RAF Tornado fighter, and giving a brief summary of the coalition's limited war aims.

Four days later the government followed the precedent set by Attlee in 1950 by itself moving a substantive motion:

> That this House expresses its full support for British forces in the Gulf and their contribution to the implementation of United Nations Resolutions by the multinational force, as authorised by United Nations Security Council Resolution 678.[9]

In an interesting development of that procedure, and with faint echoes of the events of 29 August 2013, the Opposition tabled an amendment to the government motion to add at the end:

> Commends the instructions to minimise civilian casualties wherever possible; and expresses its determination that, once the aggression in Kuwait is reversed, the United Nations and the international community must return with renewed vigour to resolving the wider problems in the Middle East.[10]

The government, sensibly (on that occasion), accepted the Opposition amendment, so that the debate could proceed as planned and the amended resolution could then be carried by the House with near unanimity.

The perennial opponents of all military adventures (including Tony Benn, Dennis Canavan and Tam Dalyell) were unhappy (or in Tam Dalyell's words 'bloody furious') about being, as they saw it, effectively prevented from voting against the war by this mechanism. Tony Benn said:

> We have had three debates on the Adjournment without substance. Today we are having a debate without choice … The point I am making is not only that different views should be expressed, but that they should be able to be tested in the lobby …[11]

Alice Mahon added:

> I deeply resent the fact that the Government have not allowed a debate to be held on going to war. I am sad that we cannot vote on the amendment.[12]

And Maria Fyfe agreed:

> I too very much regret that this House of Commons, the Mother of Parliaments has somehow not found it possible to permit a vote … This is an injustice which does nothing at all for the reputation of this Parliament … We are right to condemn the lack of democracy in some other regimes, but in doing so, it would be more fitting if we upheld standards of democracy ourselves.[13]

John Major immediately acknowledged that right, and made clear that, with a substantive motion before it, the House would indeed be able to vote. He said 'this is an occasion for hon. members to express their views, and then to vote on a substantive motion.' He was, of course, right. The House was free to, and did, vote on the substantive motion, but by adopting the sensible political expedient of accepting the Opposition's uncontroversial amendment to it, he had effectively deprived those opposed to it of the chance to register any meaningful vote against the government. As with Korea, and again with the Falklands, the mainstream of the Opposition were questioning, but wholly supportive of the government once it was embarked on war.

On this occasion the House did divide, and recorded thirty-four members voting against the substantive (amended) motion, and 563 voting in its favour. A token rebellion? Perhaps. But it may nonetheless have been one more step towards the more fundamental questioning of the Royal Prerogative before the Iraq War in 2003 and its final apparent abandonment in 2013. The significance is not that the motion supporting the war was overwhelmingly carried. That was simply adroit politics on the part of John Major (as with Clement Attlee in 1950, and in sharp contrast to the maladroit politics displayed by David Cameron on 29 August 2013). The significance is that a substantive motion allowed the House to vote on whether to support the war or not at the outset of the campaign, albeit just after its start. Just as in 1782 and 1855, and again in 1950, had the House chosen not to carry the motion the government would have had no choice but to treat it as a motion of No Confidence and either recall the troops or resign.

So the critical distinction between the exercise of the Royal Prerogative to take Britain to war on the one hand, and the exercise of Parliament's right to approve or disapprove of the decision to go to war on the other hand, was still maintained. But the gap between the two was steadily narrowing.

1998–2002 – Other Engagements Between the Two Iraq Wars: the Pressure Builds

Air strikes were ordered against Iraq in December 1998 by US and UK air forces as part of 'Operation Desert Fox', in response to Saddam Hussain's failure to comply with UN Security Council resolutions enforcing disarmament. Earlier that year there had been a substantive vote on the issue in the House of Commons, the motion reading:

That this House condemns the continuing refusal of Iraq to comply with its obligations under the relevant post-ceasefire UN Security Council Resolutions ...; believes that these programmes represent a continuing threat to international peace and stability; ... and expresses its full support also for the resolve of the Government to use all necessary means to achieve an outcome consistent with these resolutions.[14]

Tony Benn referred specifically to the use of the Royal Prerogative in going to war:

I have sat here ... through four wars – the Korean War, the Suez War, the Falklands War and the first Gulf War. I cannot remember an occasion when any government asked the House to authorise, in a resolution, action which could lead to force. The reason is that the right to go to war is a prerogative power.[15]

One would have thought he would be celebrating that fact as a welcome assertion of parliamentary control over the use of the Prerogative. But he was never so easily pleased. He added an interesting side-thought:

The Government's motion would not be carried at the Security Council. I asked the Foreign Secretary about that. Why is he asking us to pass a resolution that he could not get through the Security Council? ... Why involve the House of Commons in an act that runs counter to what the Security Council would accept?[16]

As usual, the government motion was carried by a large majority – 493 to 25, the tellers for the Noes being Mr Benn and Mr Dalyell.

Despite that straw in the wind, the Royal Prerogative again went unquestioned in 1999, when military action was undertaken to liberate Kosovo, and only afterwards

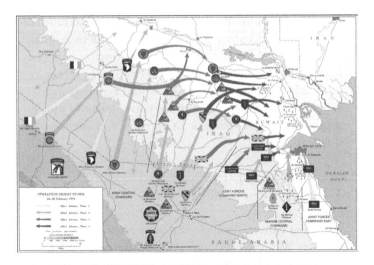

Operation Desert Storm had strengthened the 'special relationship' in 1991 and it would not be weakened by the election of a Labour government. In his first six years in government, Tony Blair ordered British troops into Iraq (in 1998 and 2003), Kosovo, Sierra Leone and Afghanistan.

were there a total of three adjournment debates to discuss the issue. But the proponents of change were increasingly starting to view this as a constitutional outrage, despite the centuries of precedent for it. Tony Benn, for example, sought to make the constitutional point by trying unsuccessfully to divide the House on the purely procedural matter of whether or not the House would adjourn IN the course of his specch he expressed the increasingly popular view that:

> ... it was wrong for British troops to be committed to war without the House of Commons discussing the matter. That is not just a constitutional question. The Government could have tabled a motion in support of their action. They did not do that because they did not think that Parliament mattered ...
>
> No amendment has been tabled ... but as in the Norway debate in 1940, we can vote against the Adjournment. [Mr Benn was not quite correct here.] I shall do that tonight, with a very heavy heart.[17]

The point of real significance about Kosovo, however, was that, in sharp contrast to Korea, the Falklands, the First Gulf War and Operation Desert Fox, there was no UN Security Council Resolution to provide legitimacy for military action. The 'coalition of the willing' had no choice but to go ahead without UN authority, because the Russians had made it clear that they would veto any such Security Council Resolution. This was the final sticking point for Tony Benn and those who held the belief that no war can ever be justified unless sanctioned by the United Nations. Later in same speech, he said:

> I have been in the Labour Party for 57 or 58 years and have been a Labour candidate seventeen times in parliamentary elections, and I never thought that I would be asked by my party to vote for a war against the Charter of the United Nations ...

It is perhaps just as well, for his own sake, that he had finally retired from the House of Commons before his party asked exactly the same of its members in 2003.

The precedent set in Kosovo in 1999 was to be oft-quoted in the run-up to Iraq in 2003, which of course equally failed to achieve UN support although an unsuccessful attempt to obtain it was made, this time on Tony Blair's insistence. Russian opposition to the putative strikes against Syria in 2013 may well have created the same dilemma for the Cameron government had the vote on 29 August gone differently.

The next major deployment of British forces abroad was in Afghanistan in late 2001, following the terrorist atrocity in New York on 11 September. Events leading up to the engagement followed the well-established pattern. Parliament was recalled from the summer recess on three separate occasions after September 11 during the run-up to operations in Afghanistan. There was an extensive adjournment debate on 14 September and then on 4 October the Prime Minister, Tony Blair, made a statement to the House of Commons, followed by a further adjournment debate, before American and British troops commenced military operations on 7 October – the Prime Minister relying in the final analysis on the Royal Prerogative to order British troops into action. So this was a further demonstration of the by now traditional procedure established as the norm since at least 1914 if not before.

During his statement to the House, the Prime Minister gave a report of the government's investigations and the conclusions reached as to the responsibility for the attack on New York and the complicity of Al Qaeda and the Taliban regime. He then said:

> I will later today put in the Library of the House of Commons a document detailing the basis for our conclusions. [But added a major caveat] much of the evidence we have is intelligence and highly sensitive. It is not possible without compromising people or security to release

precise details and fresh information is daily coming
in. But I hope the House will find it useful at least as an
interim assessment. The Leader of the Opposition and
the Leader of the Liberal Democrats have seen the full
basis for the document on Privy Council terms.[18]

This carries an interesting echo of Churchill's request
to Attlee that the House meet in secret over the Korean
deployment, and contains the seeds of the genuine worries
expressed by the more thoughtful commentators about the
level of disclosure of sensitive information which might
be needed to win a vote in a narrowly divided House over
some controversial future war. It is also significant that the
US-British intervention in Afghanistan – having been, like
Kosovo, started without UN sanction – was this time operating under the NATO umbrella.

So the route to war in Afghanistan followed the, by now,
well-established pattern of the Prime Minister, or a member
of the Cabinet, keeping the House of Commons informed
as far as practicable while fast-moving events unfolded, and
within the restraints of operational security, but the government taking the executive decision whether and when to
deploy troops and doing so by use of the Royal Prerogative.
In further accordance with precedent, on 16 October – nine
days after the start of operations – the Foreign Secretary,
Jack Straw, made a statement to the House, in which he
largely adopted, though in more modern parlance, the traditional line expounded by Balfour in August 1914 and
followed repeatedly thereafter:

> Whenever the country and the world face as grave a
> threat as they do now, the House should more than ever
> exercise its two central roles as the voice of the nation and
> as the means by which the Executive are held to account.
> In the three Prime Ministerial Statements and the three
> debates so far, there has rightly been much questioning of
> the decisions taken by Government, but the proceedings

as a whole have been characterised by the widespread
bipartisan support of our comprehensive approach.[19]

It would appear that Mr Straw had apparently either forgotten his own pledge to the Labour Party Conference
in 1994 to abolish the use of the Royal Prerogative with
regard to war-making powers, or, once in office, had come
to realise the impracticality of abolishing such a well-tried
mechanism without any clear idea of what to put in its
place – precisely the position we are now in following the
ill-thought out proceedings on 29 August 2013.

The Royal Prerogative had survived unscathed into
the twenty-first century, and remained unruffled by Tam
Dalyell finally succeeding, on 1 November 2001 and for
the first time in recent history, in dividing the House on an
adjournment motion – duly losing the vote by the usual
overwhelming majority – 373 to 13.

Thereafter, conduct of the war came under the inter-
mittent scrutiny of the House of Commons in the manner
established over the previous two centuries. On one occasion, 20 March 2002, the Conservatives used Standing
Order 24 to force the government to come to the House for
a debate on the Afghanistan deployment. Even so, Shadow
Defence Secretary, Bernard Jenkin, opened the debate
by saying:

> Our calling of this debate on the war in Afghanistan
> should not be allowed to cast any doubt on our con-
> tinuing support for the Government in the war against
> terrorism ... Let there be no doubt that we support
> the principle of that decision; but it was wrong for the
> Government to make such an announcement without
> anticipating the need for a proper debate on the subject.
> I asked the Government for a debate and they could
> have avoided the need for me to invoke Standing Order
> No. 24, but Ministers ignored our polite requests.[20]

Douglas Hogg (rather surprisingly) used this unusual procedure to propose a much more radical precedent – something quite closely akin to what appeared to be being attempted on the night of 29 August 2013, though with the important difference that he was here referring to a fresh operational deployment in an existing conflict, as opposed to the initial deployment in a conflict not yet begun. The principle however was very much the same – that Parliament should have the final say before the deployment in question was implemented. He said:

> As one who supports the deployment of British troops to Afghanistan, but one who also wants to reinforce parliamentary authority, may I say to the Right Hon. Gentleman that it would be right for the Government to come to the House and ask for an express vote authorising that deployment? Will he be so good as to say why he is not seeking the express authority of the House?[21]

But Geoff Hoon, Labour's Secretary of State for Defence, held the line on the Royal Prerogative:

> The Right Hon. and Learned Gentleman has much longer experience of this House than I. He has supported Governments who have deployed forces and has never raised that question previously … With his experience of the House, he knows that there is no automatic need for a vote. Why, then, should we take seriously such a question today?[22]

Meanwhile it was viewed as further evidence of the Labour Party's constitutional arrogance that the Prime Minister failed to attend this important debate, preferring to spend his time upstairs in a committee room discussing the future of fox hunting with the Labour Party.

Conclusions

Despite increasing involvement of Parliament by means of substantive motions of support (or otherwise) for military action at ever earlier stages, the reality is that the use of the Royal Prerogative to take the country to war was not in any real sense challenged up to and including the Afghanistan Conflict in 2001. There had been no vote on any matter of substance prior to commencement of any of the wars in question. The Opposition had consistently supported the government in the decision to go to war, and substantive debates had invariably taken place after, not before, the commencement of hostilities. Parliament continued to allow the government to take the executive decision to deploy troops, and reserved its firepower for scrutiny and criticism of the conduct of the war thereafter – with the knowledge that in the last resort it could deploy its big guns: the Censure Motion or the Vote of No Confidence. But by the time of the 2003 Iraq War the unfettered use of the Royal Prerogative was for the first time at least seriously restricted, and thereby presented a convenient precedent for whatever it was the government and the Opposition were trying unsuccessfully to do on 29 August 2013.

There is an old legal maxim of great wisdom: 'Hard cases make bad law.' And it applies with great force in this case. The decision over Iraq in 2003 must be looked at in its historical context. With the single exception of that decision (and possibly Suez in 1956) the major international conflicts in which this country has become engaged in the twentieth and twenty-first centuries have been ones in which Britain has involved itself for entirely honourable reasons and the decision to go to war has been correctly taken. Most people, we think, would agree that that applies particularly the First and Second World Wars, Korea, the Falklands, the first Gulf war, Kosovo, Sierra Leone and Afghanistan. More important, at the time they have all attracted an overwhelming measure of parliamentary support and wide general support in the country at large. And

'Whenever the country and the world face as grave a threat as they do now, the House should more than ever exercise its two central roles as the voice of the nation and as the means by which the Executive are held to account.' (Sir Arthur Balfour, August 1914)

all of them have been entered into under the tried and tested procedure of the Royal Prerogative.

So, looked at in its proper context, we arrive at a bizarre result. The system for deciding whether or not to go to war that we have developed slowly over a thousand years – the exercise of the Royal Prerogative on the decision of the Prime Minister in Cabinet, but subject to close parliamentary scrutiny thereafter - has produced a series of broadly sound decisions over the last century. The system urged upon us by the more fundamentalist reformers and the leaders of the main political parties – the total surrender of the power to decide to the will of the House of Commons – has produced what all agree was the single worst decision of modern times. That must, surely, give all serious-minded people pause for thought.

So that is the context for the momentous shambles of the night of 29 August 2013, when the Royal Prerogative to go to war appears to have been tossed rather casually onto the rubbish heap of history.

By that action a unique constitutional mechanism of great durability and flexibility, more than 1,000 years in the making – forged during the unification of England under the

Anglo-Saxons in the tenth century; developed during the emergence of Parliament as an arm of government in the Middle Ages; honed and tempered by the centralisation of power under the Tudors and the constitutional conflicts under the Stuarts; modified and partly codified by statute in the seventeenth and eighteenth centuries as Parliament moved centre stage and the beginnings of cabinet government started to emerge; flourishing through the nineteenth and twentieth centuries despite the emergence of parliamentary democracy and three cataclysmic European wars; and surviving intact into the period of popular democracy and the twenty-first century – was flung aside without any proper care or thought and, most unforgivably, without any idea at all of what to put in its place.

This is not how the British Constitution, justly renowned for its ability to adapt and grow organically as circumstances change, is supposed to be treated. We now need very urgently either to retrieve the Royal Prerogative from the rubbish heap, dust it off and consider how best to refurbish it so that the country can once again function on the international stage, or quickly come up with an equally workable, robust and durable alternative mechanism. The author of this historical section favours the former, and has hopefully provided some context to support that view. The author of the main sections of this book favours the latter, and has laid out the bones of a workable solution for consideration and debate. There may be other solutions, perhaps along the lines of the American solution provided by their War Powers Act 1973, or maybe a mixture of some or all of them.

What cannot be denied is that the machine is now broken and very urgently needs either fixing or replacing. Until it is, Britain's long and proud record as an active, positive force for freedom and order in the world will remain on hold and the respect of our allies will quickly turn to contempt as our inability to lead or take decisive action becomes ever more apparent. We owe it to those past and present who have risked or sacrificed their lives in the course of our long history not to allow it to come to such an ignoble close.

NOTES

Acknowledgements
1   *Seaford House Papers*, 2003.
2   House of Commons Library Research papers 08/88.
3   Chatham House, 2013.

Chapter 1
1   Hansard, HC Deb, Volume 566, Column 1555 (29 August 2013).
2   'Modernisation with a Purpose', Conservative Party paper, 6 February 2006.
3   Conservative Democracy Task Force, 'Power to the People', June 2007.
4   Hansard, Volume 525, Column 801 (21 March 2011).
5   Hansard, Volume 566, Column 1425 (29 August 2013).
6   Hansard, Volume 566, Column 1555 (29 August 2013).
7   Hansard, Volume 566, Column 1555 (29 August 2013).
8   'Alistair Burt reveals anger over Syria vote at Westminster' by Nicholas Watt and Patrick Wintour. *Guardian*, 30 December 2013.
9   See pp.118–121 below.

Chapter 2
1   See, for example, the fates of Lord North in 1782 (p.119 below) and Lord Aberdeen in 1855 (p.128 below).
2   Tony Benn, 'Crown Prerogatives and the House of Commons', *Tribune*, 20 August 1999.
3   Public Administration Select Committee, 'Taming the Prerogative: Strengthening Ministerial accountability to Parliament', HC 422, Session 2003-4 Ev13.
4   'This Week', BBC1, 27 Feb 2003.
5   *House Magazine*, 14 April 2003.
6   Session 2003/4, Early Day Motion 733.
7   Unpublished email from Graham Allen MP.
8   Liaison Committee, 21 January 2003.
9   Jack Straw MP, 'Abolish the Royal Prerogative' in A. Barnett, *Power and the Throne: the Monarchy Debate*, London 1994.

10 Hansard, Volume 395, Column 56, Part 1(25 November 2002).
11 Standard Note SN/1A/1218 – 'Parliament and the Use of Force', by Dr Paul Bowers.
12 Hansard, Volume 395, Column 47, Part 1 (25 November 2002).
13 Hansard, Volume 400, Part 1 (26 February 2003).
14 Hansard, Volume 401, Column 761 (18 March 2003).
15 Hansard, Volume 401, Column 761 (18 March 2003).
16 Hansard, Volume 401, Column 499W (17 March 2003).
17 Conservative Democracy Task Force, 'Power to the People', June 2007.
18 PASC Report, p.9.
19 Hansard, Volume 525, Column 613 (18 March 2011).
20 Hansard, Volume 557, Column 1055 (14 January 2013).
21 Hansard, Volume 557, Column 1054, 1059–60 (31 January 2013).
22 Hansard, Volume 595, Column 414 (9 September 2010).
23 Hansard, Volume 525, Column 801 (21 March 2011).

Chapter 5

1 It has now been announced that his report is to be published, but only with quotations from the correspondence indicating the 'gist' of them. It is to be doubted if this will satisfy the sceptics.
2 The murdering of his own people was never advanced as a justification for going to war with Hitler, the *causus belli* being the invasion of Poland, with whom we had signed a treaty of mutual assistance. The *causus belli* for the Iraq War was WMD, but again Saddam's murder of the Marsh Arabs no doubt helped to make it more palatable.

Chapter 6

1 Oxford Institute for Ethics Law and Armed Conflict, 'Operationalising the Responsibility to Protect.'

Chapter 7

1 50 U.S.C. 1541–1548.
2 P.L. 98–119.
3 Pub. L. 102–1.
4 Pub. L. 107–243.

Chapter 8

1 James de Waal, *Trusting the Right People*, Chatham House, November 2013.
2 It has now been announced that it will be published shortly.
3 *The Fog of Law: An Introduction to the Legal Erosion of British Fighting Power*, Policy Exchange, 2013.

Chapter 9
1 *Chambers Biographical Dictionary*, 5th Editon.
2 *English Historical Documents 1189-1327*, p.218.
3 Marc Morris, *A Great and Terrible King*.
4 'The Vows of the Heron', *c.* 1338, Part II.
5 The English Historical Review, No. CXVIII, Part 2.
6 Shakespeare, *The Life of King Henry the Fifth*, Act 1, Scene 2.
7 Elizabeth I, *Response to Parliamentary Delegation on Her Marriage*, 1566.
8 Letters Patent issued to Sir Francis Drake on 5 March 1587 (O.S.).
9 *Journal of the House of Commons*, Volume 1, 1547–1629.
10 Ibid.
11 *Historical Collections of Private Passages of State, Volume 1: 1618–1629.*
12 First Article of Impeachment of Thomas, Earl of Stafford.
13 The Indemnity and Oblivion Act 1660.
14 The Legal Proceedings during Commonwealth Act 1660.
15 Quoted variously, sometimes as an 'exclamation', sometimes as a diary entry.
16 The correspondence of King George III from 1760 to December 1783, from the original papers in the Royal Archives at Windsor Castle, arranged and edited by the Hon. Sir John Fortescue.

Chapter 10
1 Edmund Burke, *Reflections on the Revolution in France*, Part XI, 1790.
2 William Wordsworth, 'O pleasant exercise of hope and joy!' (1805), *Complete Poetical Works*, Macmillan.
3 Hansard, Volume 65, Column 1809 (3 August 1914).
4 Hansard, Volume 65, Column 1881–3 (3 August 1914).
5 Knowles, Elizabeth, *What They Didn't Say: A Book of Misquotations*
6 BBC Sound Archives.
7 Hansard, Volume 351, Column 293–4 (3 September 1939).
8 Screensound Australia, National Screen and Sound Collection, Screensound Title No: 387919.
9 *Canada at War* (Office of Director of Public Information of Canada) (9–20): 7. 1941.
10 Hansard, Volume 359, Column 509 (9 April 1940).

Chapter 11
1 Hansard, Volume 477, Column 485 (5 July 1950).
2 Hansard, Ibid.
3 Hansard, Volume 477, Column 495–6 (5 July 1950).

4   Hansard, Volume 557, Column 1606–7 (2 August 1956).
5   Mr Speaker Bercow now allows Private Notice Questions, now renamed Urgent Questions, on a much more regular basis as a way for backbenchers and the Opposition to hold the government to account.
6   Hansard, Volume 21, Column 965 (7 April 1982).
7   Hansard, Volume 21, Column 1022 (7 April 1982).
8   Hansard, Volume 21, Column 1177, (14 April 1982).
9   Hansard, Volume 184, Column 24 (21 January 1991).
10 Hansard, Volume 184, Column 31 (21 January 1991).
11 Hansard, Volume 184, Column 23 (21 January 1991).
12 Hansard, Volume 184, Column 49 (21 January 1991).
13 Hansard, Volume 184, Column 50 (21 January 1991).
14 Hansard, Volume 306, Column 899 (17 February 1998).
15 Hansard, Volume 306, Column 925 (17 February 1998).
16 Hansard, Ibid.
17 Hansard, Volume 328, Column 563–8 (25 March 1999).
18 Hansard, Volume 372, Column 672 (4 October 2001).
19 Hansard, Volume 372, Column 1053 (16 October 2001).
20 Hansard, Volume 382, Column 328 (20 March 2002).
21 Hansard, Volume 382, Column 333 (20 March 2002).
22 Hansard, Volume 382, Column 334 (20 March 2002).

WARS SINCE 1700

There follows a list of Britain's wars since 1700. During its history, British forces or forces with a British mandate have invaded, had some control over or fought conflicts in 171 of the 193 countries that are currently UN member states.

Kingdom of Great Britain (1707–1801)

Start	Finish	Name of Conflict	Belligerents (excluding Britain) Allies	Enemies	Outcome
1700	1721	The Great Northern War	Tsardom of Russia Kalmyk Khanate Hanover Prussia Poland–Lithuania Electorate of Saxony Cossack Hetmanate Denmark–Norway	Swedish Empire Ottoman Empire United Provinces Brunswick-Lüneburg	Coalition victory: Tsardom of Russia establishes itself as a new power in Europe Decline of Swedish Empire and the Polish–Lithuanian Commonwealth
1701	1714	The War of the Spanish Succession, including Queen Anne's War	Austria Dutch Republic Savoy Portugal Prussia	France Spain Bavaria Hungary	Treaty of Utrecht: Territory in Canada and the West Indies ceded from France Territory in Europe ceded from Spain
1715	1715	Civil War: Jacobite Rising of 1715, including the uprising in Cornwall	Government forces	Jacobites France	Jacobite restoration attempt defeated
1717	1720	The War of the Quadruple Alliance, including the Nineteen Uprising in Britain	Holy Roman Empire France Dutch Republic Savoy	Spain Jacobites (against British Crown & gov. only)	Treaty of The Hague: Spanish attempt at expansion fails
1721	1725	Dummer's War		France	Capture of Norridgewock

1740	1748	The War of the Austrian Succession, including King George's War, the War of Jenkins' Ear and the First Carnatic War	France, Prussia, Spain, French East India Company, Spanish Empire, Bavaria, Naples and Sicily, Genoa, Sweden	Austria, Hanover, Dutch Republic, Saxony, Sardinia, Russia, East India Company	Treaty of Aix-la-Chapelle: Status quo antebellum
1745	1746	Civil War: Jacobite Rising of 1745	Jacobites, France	Government forces	Jacobite restoration attempt defeated
1749	1754	The Second Carnatic War	French East India Company, Forces of Chanda Shahib, Forces of Muhyi ad-Din, Muzaffar Jang Hidayat	East India Company, Forces of Mohamed Ali Khan Walajan	Treaty of Pondicherry: Pro-British Mohamed Ali Khan Walajan became Nawab of the Carnatic
1756	1763	Seven Years' War	France, French Empire, Holy Roman Empire, Russian Empire, Sardinia, Saxony, Spain, Spanish Empire, Sweden	Prussia, Hanover, Iroquois, Portugal and her colonies, Hesse-Kassel, Brunswick-Wolfenbüttel	Treaty of Paris: Extensive North American lands (incl. all of Canada) ceded from France, Caribbean colonies ceded from France, Senegal River colony (excluding Gorée) ceded from France, Florida ceded from Spain

				France	
1757	1763	The Third Carnatic War	East India Company	French East India Company	Treaty of Paris: French trading posts in India administered by British Sumatra ceded from France
1758	1761	Anglo-Cherokee War		Cherokee	Pro-British Attakullakulla becomes Cherokee leader
1763	1766	Pontiac's Rebellion		Confederation of First Nation Tribes	Stalemate: British policy change British suzerainty over First Nation Tribes Niagara Falls area ceded from Seneca Nation
1766	1769	First Anglo-Mysore War	East India Company Hyderabad State Maratha Empire	Kingdom of Mysore	British defeat, Hyderabad cedes territory to Mysore
1774	1783	First Anglo-Maratha War	East India Company	Maratha Empire	Treaty of Salbai: Salsette Island ceded from Maratha Empire Territory west of Jumna River ceded to Maratha Empire Maratha support for Britain against Mysore
1775	1783	American Revolutionary War. American War of Independence, including: Anglo-French War, Anglo-Spanish War,	Iroquois Cherokee Hanover Loyalists	United States France Spain Catawba tribe Dutch Republic	Treaty of Paris: 13 British colonies granted independence as the United States. Territory in North America ceded to new United States

		Fourth Anglo-Dutch War		Watauga Association Vermont Republic Kingdom of Mysore Tuscarora tribe Oneida tribe	Senegal River colony returned to France France recognises British suzerainty over the Gambia River Territory in India returned to France Minorca ceded to Spain East & West Florida ceded to Spain All British settlers to be expelled from Florida Demilitarisation of British Honduras Territory in India ceded by the Dutch
1780	1784	2nd Anglo-Mysore War	East India Company Maratha Empire Hyderabad State	Kingdom of Mysore	Treaty of Mangalore: Status quo antebellum
1789	1792	3rd Anglo-Mysore War	East India Company Maratha Empire Hyderabad State Travancore	Kingdom of Mysore France	Treaty of Seringapatnam: Half of Mysore territory ceded to East India Company
1793	1797	The War of the First Coalition	Austria Prussia French Royalists Spain Kingdom of Portugal Kingdom of Sardinia Dutch Republic Naples and Sicily Italian states Ottoman Empire	French Republic French satellite states Polish Legions	Treaty of Campo Formio. Survival of the French Republic French annexation of the Austrian Netherlands Several French client republics established Britain remained at war with France into the War of the Second Coalition, ending with the Treaty of Amiens

			French Royalists	French Republic	British-backed rebellion defeated
1793	1796	War in the Vendée	French Royalists	French Republic	British-backed rebellion defeated
1795	1816	Hawkesbury and Nepean Wars	Loyalists Burrberongai Tribe	Dharug Eora Tharawal Gandangara Irish-convict sympathisers	British Victory Displacement of Aborigines from their land
1798	1798	Irish Rebellion of 1798	Hesse-Homburg	United Irishmen Defenders French Republic	Rebellion defeated 1801 Act of Union
1798	1799	4th Anglo-Mysore War	East India Company Hyderabad State Maratha Empire	Kingdom of Mysore French Republic	Complete annexation of Mysore by Britain and allies
1799	1802	War of the Second Coalition	Austria Russia French Royalists Portugal Two Sicilies Ottoman Empire	French Republic Spain Polish Legions French client republics: Parthenopaean Republic Roman Republic Batavian Republic Helvetic Republic Cisalpine Republic	Treaty of Amiens: General French victory Britain recognises the French Republic Cape Colony returned to the French client, Batavian Republic French withdrawal from Egypt French withdrawal from the Papal States Trinidad and Tobago ceded from France Ceylon ceded from the Batavian Republic

United Kingdom of Great Britain and Ireland (1801–1922)

Start	Finish	Name of Conflict	Belligerents (excluding Britain) Allies	Enemies	Outcome
1801	1807	Temne War	Susu tribes	Kingdom of Koya	Northern shore of Sierra Leone ceded by Koya
1802	1805	Second Anglo-Maratha War	East India Company	Maratha Empire	Extensive territory in India ceded by the Maratha Empire
1803	1805	First Kandyan War		Kandy	Territory captured from Kandy
1803	1803	Civil War Emmet's Insurrection	Loyalists	Forces of Robert Emmet	Rebellion defeated
1803	1805	War of the Third Coalition	Austrian Empire Russian Empire Naples and Sicily Portugal Sweden	French Empire Batavia Italy Etruria Spain Württemberg Bavaria	Fourth Peace of Preßburg: French victory Austria surrenders to France Pro-French Confederation of the Rhine formed
1806	1807	War of the Fourth Coalition	Prussia Russia Saxony Sweden Sicily	French Empire Confederation of the Rhine Swiss Confederation Bavaria Spain Württemberg Polish Legions	Treaties of Tilsit: French victory Half of Prussia ceded to French allies Russia exits the war Anglo-Russian War begins

			Italy Naples Etruria Holland		
1806	1807	British invasions of the Rio de la Plata		Spain River Plate Viceroyalty	Invasion defeated
1806	1807	Ashanti–Fante War	Ashanti Empire	Fante Confederacy Dutch Empire	Rebel leader handed over to Ashanti
1807	1809	Anglo-Turkish War		Ottoman Empire	Treaty of the Dardanelles: Turkish victory Commercial and legal concessions to British interests within the Ottoman Empire Promise to protect the empire against French encroachment
1807	1814	Gunboat War.		Denmark-Norway	Treaty of Kiel: Denmark and Norway split up Heligoland ceded from Denmark
1807	1812	Anglo-Russian War.		Russian Empire	Treaty of Örebro: Anglo-Russian–Swedish pact against France
1807	1814	Peninsular War.	Spain Portugal	French Empire	1st Treaty of Paris: Bourbon dynasty restored Tobago, St. Lucia, Mauritius ceded from France.

1809	1809	War of the Fifth Coalition.	Austrian Empire Tyrol Hungary Black Brunswickers Sicily Sardinia	French Empire Warsaw Confederation of the Rhine Holland Bavaria Saxony Württemberg Westphalia Kingdom of Italy Naples Swiss Confederation	Treaty of Schönbrunn: Complete Austrian surrender Peninsular War continued All other French possessions restored as per 1792 borders Abolition of French Slave Trade Swiss independence
1810	1817	Merina Conquest of Madagascar.	Merina Kingdom	French Empire	Merina control of Madagascar Merina pro-British policies
1811	1812	4th Xhosa War.		Xhosa tribes	Xhosa tribes pushed beyond the Fish River, reversing their gains in the previous Xhosa wars
1811	1811	Ga-Fante War.	Ashanti Empire Dutch Empire Ga tribes	Fante Confederacy Akim tribes Akwapim tribes	Tantamkweri ceded to Akwapim tribes
1812	1815	War of 1812	Province of Upper Canada Province of Lower Canada	United States	Treaty of Ghent: Status quo antebellum

		War			Outcome
1815	1815	Second Kandyan War	Kandy		Kandyan Convention: Dissolution of the Kandy royal line; British King declared King of Kandy
1815	1815	Hundred Days' War, War of the Seventh Coalition	French Empire; Naples	Portugal, France, Hanover, Tuscany, German Confederation, Kingdom of the Two Sicilies, Austria, Sardinia, Russia, Sweden, Netherlands, Spain	2nd Treaty of Paris: Restoration of the House of Bourbon; Abolition of the slave trade (all signatories); 100,000,000 francs compensation from France
1817	1818	Third Anglo-Maratha War	Maratha Empire	East India Company	Virtually all territory south of the Sutlej River controlled by Britain
1818	1819	5th Xhosa War	Forces of Xhosa Chief Maqana Nxele	Khoikhoi Forces	Xhosa pushed beyond Keiskama River
1820	1830	Greek War of Independence	Ottoman Empire; Egypt	Greek revolutionaries; Ionian Islands	Establishment of the Kingdom of Greece
1823	1831	First Ashanti War	Ashanti Empire		British retreat to Sierra Leone; New borders agreed with Ashanti Empire

1824	1826	First Anglo-Burmese War	East India Company / Native tribes	Kingdom of Burma	Treaty of Yandabo: / Assam, Manipur, Rakhine, and Taninthayi coast south of Salween River ceded from Burma / £1,000,000 compensation from Burma
1828	1834	Portuguese Civil War	Liberal Forces of Queen Maria II / Spain	Absolutist Forces of King Miguel	Concession of Evoramonte: / Defeat and exile of King Miguel
1833	1840	First Carlist War	Forces of Queen Isabella II / Forces of Queen Maria II / French Kingdom	Carlists: / Forces of King Miguel / Forces of Infante Carlos	British mediated Convention of Vergara
1834	1836	The 6th Xhosa War	Free Khoikhoi	Xhosa tribes	Extensive territorial gains from Xhosa
1837	1838	Rebellions of 1837	Province of Upper Canada / Province of Lower Canada	Patriot movement / American Volunteers / Republic of Canada / Hunters' Lodges	Rebellion defeated / Report on the Affairs of British North America: / Pro-French policy in Québec ended / Lower and Upper Canada merged into single province
1839	1842	First Anglo-Afghan War	East India Company	Emirate of Afghanistan	British retreat from Afghanistan
1839	1842	First Opium War		Manchu-China	Treaty of Nanking: / Five Chinese ports open to foreign trade / $21,000,000 compensation from the Qing Empire / Hong Kong Island ceded from the Qing Empire
1839	1851	Uruguayan Civil War	Colorados / Italian Legion	Blancos / Argentine Confederation	British and French withdrawal before war's conclusion / Peace treaty with the Argentine Confederation

					Eventual Colorados victory
			Argentine Unitarians / Brazil / French Kingdom / Riograndense Republic		
1845	1846	First Anglo-Sikh War	East India Company / Patiala State	Sikh Empire	Treaty of Lahore: / Extensive territory ceded from the Sikh Empire / Partial control over Sikh foreign affairs
1845	1846	Flagstaff War	Forces of Tāmati Wāka Nene	Ngāpuhi Iwi	Stalemate
1846	1846	Hutt Valley Campaign	Te Āti Awa Iwi	Ngāti Toa Iwi	Ngāti Toa Iwi retreat
1846	1847	The 7th Xhosa War, / The War of the Axe		Xhosa tribes	Territory ceded from Xhosa
1847	1847	Wanganui Campaign	Māori Kupapa	Māori Iwis	Stalemate / 12 year peace and trade
1848	1849	Second Anglo-Sikh War	East India Company	Sikh Empire	Complete annexation of the Punjab by the East India Company
1851	1853	The 8th Xhosa War, / Mlanjeni's War		Xhosa tribes / Khoikhoi tribes / Native Kafir Police	Xhosa-Khoi attacks defeated / Status quo antebellum
1852	1853	Second Anglo-Burmese War		Kingdom of Burma	Burmese revolution ended fighting / Lower Burma annexed

1853	1856	Crimean War	French Empire Ottoman Empire Kingdom of Sardinia	Russian Empire Bulgarian Legion	Treaty of Paris
1856	1857	National War in Nicaragua	Costa Rica The Mosquito Coast Honduras Rebel Forces of Patricio Rivas	Sonora Nicaragua	American-Nicaraguan government defeated Slavery outlawed
1856	1860	Second Opium War, Arrow War	French Empire United States	Manchu-China	The Treaty of Tientsin: Kowloon ceded from the Qing Empire Peking opened to foreign trade 11 more Chinese ports opened to foreign trade Yangtze River opened to foreign warships 4,000,000 taels of silver compensation China banned from referring to subjects of the crown as barbarians
1856	1857	Anglo-Persian War	Afghanistan East India Company	Persia Herat	Persian withdrawal from Herat
1857	1858	Indian Mutiny	East India Company Sepoys of the EIC armies of Bombay and Madras Nepal Sikh Princes Jammu and Kashmir	Sepoys of the EIC army of Bengal Mughal Empire Awadh Jhansi Oudh	Act for the Better Government of India: Company rule in India dissolved Indian Empire established Ban on Christian missionaries in India

			Allies	Opponents	Outcome
			Princely states: Rewa Ajaigarh Hyderabad Mysore Kendujhar Jaipur Bikaner Marwar Rampur Kapurthala Nabha Bhopal Sirohi Udaipur Patiala Sirmur Alwar Bharathpur Bundi Jaora Bijawar	Princely states: Jhajjar Dadri Farukhnagar Bahadurgha Amjera Shagarth Biaj Raghodahr Singhbum Nargund Shorapur	
1860	1861	First Taranaki War, Second Māori War		Māori iwis Māori King Movement	Stalemate
1863	1864	Second Ashanti War		Ashanti Empire	Stalemate
1863	1866	Invasion of Waikato, Third Māori War	Māori Kupapa	Māori King Movement	Māori King Movement defeated, confined to King Country

1864	1865	Bhutan War	India	Bhutan	Treaty of Sinchula: Bhutan cedes Assam Duars and Bengal Duars to India / Bhutan cedes territory in Dewangiri to India
1867	1874	Klang War, Selangor Civil War	Forces of Raja Abdullah of Klang / British Straits Settlements	Forces of Raja Mahadi	
1868	1869	Titokowaru's War, part of the New Zealand land wars	Māori Kupapa	Ngāti Ruanui Iwi	Ngāti Ruanui Iwi withdrawal
1868	1868	1868 Expedition to Abyssinia	India	Abyssinia	British hostages freed / War of the Abyssinian Succession begins
1868	1872	Te Kooti's War, part of the New Zealand land wars	Māori Kupapa	Māori Iwis	End of New Zealand land wars / Territory ceded by Māori Iwis
1869	1869	Red River Rebellion	Dominion of Canada / Métis Loyalists	Métis Forces of Louis Riel	Defeat of rebellion / Manitoba Act: / Creation of the Province of Manitoba
1873	1874	Third Ashanti War		Ashanti Empire	Treaty of Fomena: / 50,000oz of gold compensation from Ashanti Empire / Ashanti withdrawal from coastal areas / Ashanti banned from practising human sacrifice

1877	1878	The 9th Xhosa War	Mfengu Tribe	Xhosa Gcaleka Tribe	All Xhosa territory annexed to the Cape Colony
1878	1880	Second Anglo-Afghan War	India	Afghanistan	British control over Afghan foreign affairs
1879	1879	Anglo-Zulu War	Natal	Zulu Kingdom	Zululand annexed to Natal
1880	1881	First Boer War		South African Republic	Pretoria Convention: South African Republic granted self-government
1884	1889	Mahdist War	Egypt Belgium Italy	Mahdist Sudan	Sudan ruled by Britain and Egypt
1885	1885	Third Anglo-Burmese War		Kingdom of Burma	Upper Burma annexed to British Raj
1888	1888	Sikkim Expedition	India	Tibet	Tibet recognises British suzerainty over Sikkim
1896	1896	Anglo-Zanzibar War		Zanzibar	Pro-British Sultan installed
1899	1901	Boxer Rebellion	Japan Russia France Austria-Hungary United States Germany Italy	Righteous Harmony Society Manchu-China	Boxer Protocol: Anti-foreign societies banned in China
1899	1902	Second Boer War		Orange Free State	Treaty of Vereeniging:

1901	1902	Anglo-Aro War	South African Republic Foreign volunteers	Aro Confederacy	All Boers to surrender arms and swear allegiance to the Crown Dutch language permitted in education Promise to grant Boer republic self-government. £3,000,000 compensation 'reconstruction aid' to Afrikaners Aro Confederacy destroyed
1903	1904	British expedition to Tibet	India	Tibet	Status quo antebellum
1914	1918	First World War	India Dominion of Canada Dominion of Australia Dominion of New Zealand Dominion of South Africa Newfoundland United States Italy France Belgium Russia Greece Portugal Romania Japan Montenegro Serbia Other Allies	Austria-Hungary Germany German Empire Ottoman Empire Bulgaria	Treaty of Versailles: German demobilisation Treaties of Saint-Germain-en-Laye and Trianon: Demise of Austria-Hungary Russia pulls out in 1917 Russian Civil War Creation of the Soviet Union Stalin rises to power Creation of League of Nations Mesopotamia ceded from the Ottoman Empire Palestine and Jordan ceded from the Ottoman Empire Tanganyika ceded from Germany

					Part of Kamerun ceded from Germany Part of Togoland ceded from Germany German New Guinea ceded to Australia German Samoa ceded to New Zealand German South-west Africa ceded to South Africa
1918	1920	Allied intervention in the Russian Civil War	British Empire France United States Greece Japan White Russians	Soviet Russia Far Eastern Republic	Allied withdrawal from Russia Bolshevik victory over White Army Soviet Union new Russian power Stalin rises to power
1919	1923	Turkish War of Independence	Greece France Italy Armenia	Turkish Nationalists	Treaty of Lausanne: Turkish Nationalist victory British withdrawal End of the Ottoman Empire
1919	1919	Third Anglo-Afghan War	India	Afghanistan	Full Afghan independence
1919	1921	Irish War of Independence	Loyalists	Irish Republic	Anglo-Irish Treaty: Dominion status for southern Ireland as the Irish Free State
1920	1920	Somaliland campaign	British Somaliland British East Africa	Dervish State	Demise of the Dervish State
1920	1920	Great Iraqi Revolution		Iraqi rebels	Revolt suppressed, greater autonomy given to Iraq

United Kingdom of Great Britain and Northern Ireland (1922–present)

Start	Finish	Name of Conflict	Belligerents (excluding Britain) Allies	Enemies	Outcome
1936	1939	Great Arab Revolt in Palestine	Jewish Settlement Police Jewish Supernumerary Police Haganah Special Night Squads FOSH Peulot Meyuhadot Irgun Peace Bands	Arab Higher Committee	Revolt suppressed
1938	1948	British–Zionist conflict	Lehi	Haganah Irgun Palmach	British withdrawal and creation of Israel
1939	1945	Second World War	The Allies: France Poland Belgium Netherlands Luxembourg Czechoslovakia Norway Greece Yugoslavia	Axis Powers: Germany Vichy France Thailand Finland Mengjiang Manchukuo Romania Croatia Bulgaria	Total defeat for Axis Powers British, French, American, andSoviet troops occupy Germany until 1955 Italy and Japan lose all of their colonies

Start	End	Conflict	Allies	Opponents	Notes
			United States, USSR, China, Brazil, South Africa, Nepal, India, New Zealand, Canada, Australia	Italy, Japan, Hungary	
1945	1949	Indonesian National Revolution	Netherlands, Japan (Until 1945)	Indonesia	Netherlands recognises Indonesian independence
1944	1948	Greece (Greek Civil War)	Kingdom of Greece, USA	Albania, Yugoslavia, Bulgaria, Soviet Union	Britain withdraws most support from March 1947; US provides support; Greek government overcomes revolt; At least 1 battalion of UK troops still in Greece by 1948
1945	1946	Vietnam (Operation Masterdom)	India, Japan, France	Viet Minh	First Indochina War begins
1948	1960	Malayan Emergency	Malaya, Australia, Kenya, United Nations, New Zealand, Southern Rhodesia, Fiji	Malayan Communist Party, Malayan Races Liberation Army	Communist retreat from Malaya; Malayan independence

1950	1953	Korean War	South Korea United States Canada Australia New Zealand	North Korea People's Republic of China Soviet Union	Stalemate: Communist invasion of South Korea defeated UN invasion of North Korea repulsed
1951	1954	Suez Canal Zone Emergency			Agreement for Britain to withdraw from Canal zone Bases, last British troops left June 1956
1952	1960	Mau Mau Uprising	British East Africa	Mau Mau	Defeat of Mau Mau Kenyan independence
1955	1960	Cyprus Emergency		EOKA	Independence of Cyprus
1956	1957	Suez Crisis	France Israel	Egypt	Israeli occupation of Sinai Anglo-French withdrawal
1956	1962	Border Campaign		Irish Republican Army	IRA campaign fails
1962	1966	Indonesia–Malaysia confrontation	Malaysia Australia New Zealand	Indonesia	Indonesia recognises Malaysian rule over former North Borneo
1962	1975	Dhofar Rebellion	Oman Iran Jordan	Various insurgents	Insurgency defeated Modernisation of Oman
1963	1967	Aden Emergency	Federation of South Arabia	NLF FLOSY	British withdrawal People's Republic of South Yemen established

				Republican paramilitaries / Unionist paramilitaries	Good Friday Agreement: Devolution in Northern Ireland Power-sharing deal
1968	1998	The Troubles			
1982	1982	Falklands War		Argentina	Falklands Islands are retaken from Argentina, South Georgia and the South Sandwich Islands are retaken from Argentina
1982	1984	Multinational Force in Lebanon	France United States Italy	Syria	Britain provides smaller contribution than the other 3 powers from Feb 1983; the 3 others had intervened in Aug 1982 Britain, US, and Italy leave in Feb 1984, with the French leaving by Mar 31 1984
1991	1991	Gulf War	Kuwait Other Allies United States Saudi Arabia France Egypt Syria	Iraq	Kuwait regains its independence
1992	1996	Bosnian War	NATO	Republika Srpska	Dayton Accords
1998	1998	Operation Desert Fox	United States	Iraq	Ceasefire Objectives largely achieved

1998	1999	Kosovo War	United States Kosovo Liberation Army France Italy Germany Canada Denmark	Yugoslavia	Kosovo occupied by Nato forces Kosovo administered by UNMIK
2000	2002	Sierra Leone Civil War	Sierra Leone	Rebels Liberia	Rebels defeated
2001		War in Afghanistan, Fourth Anglo-Afghan War	Afghanistan United States ISAF Spain Canada Australia Germany Italy France Poland Romania Turkey	Islamic Emirate of Afghanistan	Fall of Taliban regime Osama bin Laden killed Ongoing Taliban insurgency
2003	2009	Iraq War	United States Iraq after the fall of Saddam Hussein Australia Poland Denmark	Iraq under Saddam Hussein Various insurgents Iraqi Kurdistan	Fall of Ba'athist rule in Iraq Occupation of southern Iraq British withdrawal in 2009, conflict ended in 2011

| 2011 | 2011 | Libyan Intervention | Many NATO members acting under UN mandate, including:
United States
France
Sweden
Anti-Gaddafi forces
Canada
Italy
Several Arab League states | Pro-Gaddafi forces | Fall of Gaddafi regime
Muammar Gaddafi killed
National Transitional Council take control |

BIBLIOGRAPHY

The Cambridge History of English and American Literature Vol. II – The End of the Middle Ages (for quotations from 'The Vows of the Heron').

Catchpole, Brian, *The Korean War 1950–1953* (Constable & Robinson Ltd, 2000) (and Magpie Books, 2010).

Chambers Biographical Dictionary, 5th Edition (W & R Chambers Ltd, 1990)

De Waal, James, *Depending on the Right People, British Political–Military Relations, 2001–10* (Chatham House, November 2013).

Douglas, David C. (gen. ed.), Harry Rothwell (ed.),*English Historical Documents 1189–1327* (Eyre & Spottiswoode, 1975) (and Routledge, 1996).

Gray, James, 'Crown vs Parliament: Who decides on going to War?' (RCDS thesis printed as *Seaford House Papers*, 2003).

Hague, William, *William Pitt the Younger* (Harper Collins, 2004).

Hastings, Max, *Catastrophe: Europe Goes to War 1914* (William Collins, 2013).

House of Lords Select Committee on the Constitution, *Fifteenth Report of Session 2005–6: Waging War: Parliament's Role and Responsibility.*

Howarth, David, *1066: The Year of Conquest* (Penguin Books, 1981).

Knowles, Elizabeth, *What They Didn't Say: A Book of Misquotations* (Oxford University Press, 2006)

Mattingly, Garrett, *The Defeat of the Spanish Armada* (Jonathan Cape 1959) (and Pimlico Edition, 2000).

Ministry of Justice, Ministry of Defence and Foreign & Commonwealth Office Consultation Paper, 2007, *War Powers and Treaties: Limiting Executive Powers.*

Morris, Marc, *A Great and Terrible King: Edward I and the Forging of Britain* (Hutchinson, 2008).

Mortimer, Ian, *The Perfect King: A Life of Edward III, the Father of the English Nation* (Jonathan Cape, 2006) (and Vintage, 2008).

'Opposition Day Debate on Armed Conflict (Parliamentary Approval)', 15 May 2007 (Hansard, Col 481).

Phillipson, Gavin, 'Historic Commons' Syria vote: the Constitutional Significance'. (UK Constitutional Law Association Blog, 29 November 2013).

Political and Constitutional Reform Committee's Eighth Report of Session 2010–12, *Parliament's Role in Conflict Decisions.*

Public Administration Select Committee Fourth Report of Session 2003–4, *Taming the Prerogative: Strengthening Ministerial Accountability to Parliament.*

Royle, Trevor, *Crimea: The Great Crimean War 1854–1856* (Little Brown & Company, 1999) (and Abacus, 2000).

Taylor, Claire, and Richard Kelly, House of Commons Library, *Parliamentary Approval for deploying the Armed Forces: An Introduction to the Issues* (November 2008) (and updated, February 2013).

Towle, Philip, *Going to War. British Debates from Wilberforce to Blair* (Palgrave Macmillan, 2006).

Tughendhat, Thomas, and Laura Croft, *The Fog of Law: An Introduction to the Legal Erosion of British Fighting Power* (Policy Exchange, 2013).

Wedgwood, C.V., *The King's Peace 1637–1641* (Collins, 1955; then the Folio Society by arrangement with the Principal and Fellows of Lady Margaret Hall, Oxford, 2001).

The following volumes of the *Oxford History of England*:

Anglo-Saxon England by Sir Frank Stenton.

Thirteenth Century 1216–1307 by Sir Maurice Powicke.

Fourteenth Century 1307–1399 by May McKisack.

The Reign of Elizabeth 1558–1603 by J.B. Black.

The Early Stuarts 1603–1660 by Godfrey Davies.

The Later Stuarts 1660–1714 by Sir George Clark.

The Whig Supremacy 1714–1760 by Basil Williams, revised by C.H. Stuart.

The Reign of George III 1760–1815 by J. Steven Watson.

Age of Reform 1815–1870 by Sir Llewellyn Woodward.

England 1870–1914 by Sir Robert Ensor.

English History 1914–1945 by A.J.P. Taylor.

ABOUT THE AUTHORS

James Gray has been the MP for North Wiltshire since 1997. A former Shadow Defence Minister (resigned over Iraq), he is a member of the House of Commons Defence Select Committee, Chairman of the All Party Parliamentary Group for the Armed Forces and the Armed Forces Parliamentary Trust. He served for seven years (as a humble gunner) in the Honourable Artillery Company and subsequently on its Court of Assistants, and was a Visiting Parliamentary Fellow of St Anthony's College Oxford in 2006. His previous books include: *Shipping Futures* (Lloyds of London Book Prize, 1986); 'Crown vs Parliament: Who decides on going to War?' (Royal College of Defence Studies prize, *Seaford House Papers*, 2003) and *Poles Apart* (2013). A Scot by birth and background, James was educated at Glasgow University and Christ Church, Oxford. A career in the City preceded politics. He and his wife, Philippa, live in North Wiltshire.

Mark Lomas was called to the Bar at the Middle Temple in 1977 and took silk in 2003. He practised for thirty-two years at the Common Law and Commercial Bar, specialising in professional negligence and insurance matters. He sits as a commercial arbitrator in insurance disputes and became an accredited commercial mediator in 2001. In 2009 he gave up practice as an advocate to devote himself full time to his practice as an arbitrator and mediator. He served for several years (as a humble trooper) in the Honourable Artillery

Company. He was educated at Oundle, and Trinity Hall, Cambridge, where he read history and developed a lasting, though strictly amateur, interest in English constitutional history. He and his late wife, Jo, a talented event rider, lived in Leicestershire until her sudden death in a riding accident in 2012 at the age of 49. He now lives in London.

INDEX

Offices given are for the period under discussion when the person is first named.